Congress and the Federal Budget

Congress and the Federal Budget

FEDERAL BUDGETING

The Choice of Government Programs

By

Murray L. Weidenbaum

★ ★ ★

THE RESPONSIBLE USE OF POWER

A Critical Analysis of the Congressional Budget Process

By

John S. Saloma III

FOREWORD

Each January when the President sends his Budget Message to Congress much interest—and not a little confusion—develops across the country in the financial affairs of the National Government and how they affect the citizen and taxpayer. One hears and reads figures of different amounts for what seem to be the same things. Terms such as "new obligational authority," "authorizations," "Appropriations," "administrative budget," "Cash budget," and national income budget" are encountered. When resort is made to the budget documents themselves, little help is found (though the Bureau of the Budget has made great efforts in recent years to make the budget more meaningful and useful by publishing a summary "Budget in Brief" and by separating from the budget itself an appendix containing the detailed statistics). Beyond those specialists in and out of government who work with the budget and follow federal fiscal affairs in some detail, there is little understanding of the procedures by which the budget is prepared or how the Congress acts upon it.

With these problems in mind, the two studies presented in *Congress and the Federal Budget* deal with budget preparation, explanation, and handling in Congress.

Professor Murray L. Weidenbaum is the author of "Federal Budgeting: The Choice of Government Programs." Professor Weidenbaum, presently on the faculty of Washington University in St. Louis, was formerly with the Federal Bureau of the Budget and has worked extensively in the fields of governmental administration, budgeting, and expenditure. In his study he examines the preparation of the federal budget and the review of it in the Congress. Professor Weidenbaum indicates several lines of potential improvement in both preparation and review. Pointing out that the central problem in budgeting is primarily the choice of government programs, a framework is suggested for preparation of the federal budget which would permit greater choice among the various alternative government programs and a more deliberate and systematic allocation of budget funds among the major purposes of government.

"The Responsible Use of Power: A Critical Analysis of the Congressional Budget Process" is by Professor John S. Saloma, III. Dr. Saloma is assistant professor of political science at the Massachusetts Institute of Technology, and a former Congressional Fellow. For some time he has been concerned with congressional reorganization. His study is an analysis of the congressional role in the budget process. Its primary focus is the authorization-appropriations phase of budgeting, although it also is concerned with revenue actions, the congressional review function in the expenditure of funds, and the broader economic implications of congressional budgetary decisions. Professor Saloma traces the development of legislative and executive roles in the budgetary process and indicates several lines of potential improvement in congressional handling of the budget.

Each of these studies was published separately during 1964. In view of their complementary nature, they have been bound together under one cover. AEI hopes these two studies will be useful to all those interested in the fiscal affairs of the Federal Government.

THOMAS F. JOHNSON
Director of Research

March 1965

CONTENTS

FOREWORD vii

    By THOMAS F. JOHNSON
     Director of Research
     American Enterprise Institute
     for Public Policy Research

FEDERAL BUDGETING
    The Choice of Government Programs

    By MURRAY L. WEIDENBAUM
     Senior Economist
     Stanford Research Institute

INTRODUCTION 1

THE PRESSURES FOR GOVERNMENT SPENDING 5
    Concentration of Expenditures by Function 7
    Regional Concentrations of Federal Expenditures . . . 10
    Concentration by Industry 15
    Some Observations 17

FEDERAL SPENDING AND THE LOCALITY 19
    Grants and Matching Funds 20
    Direct Federal Expenditures 21
    Loans and Advances 21
    Insuring and Leaseback Programs 21
    Comments 22

THE MECHANICS OF GOVERNMENT SPENDING 25
    Basic Authorizing Legislation 26
    Requests for New Funds 28
    Congressional Enactment of Appropriations 29
    New Obligational Authority 33
    Apportionment of Funds 34
    Incurring Obligations 35

Making Payments 35
Reducing Governmental Spending 36
The Points of Control 38

THE BUILT-IN RIGIDITIES IN THE FEDERAL BUDGET 41
Department of Health, Education, and Welfare 42
Department of the Interior 45
Other Agencies 46
Need for Congressional Review of Fixed Budget Items 49

PROPOSED LEGISLATION:
    BIRTH STAGE OF GOVERNMENT SPENDING 53

THE CHOICE AMONG ALTERNATIVES 59
National Security 61
Public Welfare 62
Economic Development 64
Government Operations 66
Utilization of the Purpose Approach 66
The Choice of Not to Spend 69

THE SEARCH FOR IMPROVEMENTS IN
    BUDGET-CONTROL TECHNIQUES 71
Organization for Budgetary Control 72
Congressional Procedures 74
Suggested Mechanism to Assist in Budget Review . . 76
Choice of Budget Concept 81

SUMMARY AND CONCLUSIONS 85
The Concentration of Pressures 85
The Mechanics of Government Spending 86
Built-In Rigidities 87
The Choice Among Alternatives 88
Improvements in Budget-Control Techniques 89

APPENDIX A 91

APPENDIX B 95

BIBLIOGRAPHY 101

THE RESPONSIBLE USE OF POWER:
A Critical Analysis of the Congressional Budget Process

By JOHN S. SALOMA III
Assistant Professor of Political Science
Massachusetts Institute of Technology

INTRODUCTION 103

THE CONGRESSIONAL BUDGET PROCESS 107
    Legislative and Executive Roles in the Budget Process 108
    Major Characteristics of the Congressional Budget
        Process 120

COMMON CRITICISMS OF THE CONGRESSIONAL BUDGET
    PROCESS 129

CONGRESSIONAL INITIATIVE: MAJOR ATTEMPTS TO
    REFORM THE CONGRESSIONAL BUDGETARY SYSTEM 143
    Congressional Utilization of the General Accounting
        Office 144
    Staffing the Appropriations Committees 151
    Congressional Attempts to Establish a Legislative
        Budget 160
    The Omnibus Appropriations Bill 164
    The Joint Committee on the Budget 169

A STRATEGY FOR FISCAL REFORM—GOALS,
    LIMITATIONS, AND RECOMMENDATIONS 175
    The Choice of Goals 176
    The Limitation to Reform 179
    Recommendations for Reforming the Congressional
        Budgetary System 181
    A Postscript on Expectations 193

FIGURES 195
    I. Major Steps in the Budget Process 196
    II. Components of the Congressional Budget Process 198
    III. Relationship of Congressional Authorization ... 200
    IV. Staffs of the House and Senate Committees on
        Appropriations 202

INDEX 205

FEDERAL BUDGETING
THE CHOICE OF GOVERNMENT PROGRAMS

By

MURRAY L. WEIDENBAUM

INTRODUCTION

The Budget, Strange Fish and Monster Vast
To Which from All Sides the Hook is Cast.
—Victor Hugo

IN THE OFFICE of one former director of the Bureau of the Budget, there once hung a chart entitled, "The Tools of Budgeting." Three such tools were portrayed—crystal ball, some dice, and a pair of scissors.

It well may be that these items still represent the most realistic techniques for preparing and reviewing budgetary recommendations. Nevertheless, this study attempts to supply more formal methodology to the process.

Essentially, the purpose is to demonstrate how some relatively simple economic concepts can be applied toward the achievement of improved allocations of government funds among alternative uses. It is hoped that the central problem of budgeting will thus be highlighted; namely, the choice of government programs.

This study of Federal Government spending is based on the belief that—despite all of the well-intentioned attempts to reduce budgeted expenditures or otherwise reform or modify the presidential budgetary recommendations—many of the efforts are unsuccessful for one or both of the following reasons:

1. Lack of a proper public understanding as to how the budgetary system works in practice, particularly with respect to the mechanism for funding government programs and the methods of review and control which it offers, and

2. Lack on the part of the Congress of effective budget-reviewing tools and mechanisms to assist it toward wise decisions in the determination of the amounts of public funds that should be expended and in the allocation of these funds among the various government programs.

For the purpose of appraising means for overcoming these obstacles, this study first offers an explanation of the pressures for instituting, maintaining, and expanding government spending programs. It is demonstrated that the usual situation is for any given government spending program to have a specific group of supporters who think they benefit more from the government expenditure than they would from the general tax reduction which might be permitted by the elimination of the program.

The next section describes the sequences of the government spending process, particularly highlighting the key points of control, some of which are not generally considered to be parts of the budgetary process itself. These latter control points include the enactment by the Congress of basic legislation authorizing government programs to be carried on and the apportionment and allotment of funds by Executive Branch officials.

Subsequently, by way of a case study, a detailed analysis is undertaken of the 1964 budget prepared by the President. This review shows the substantial limitations that exist as to the proportion of the federal budget which may be subjected to effective congressional review and control each year through the appropriating process. For example, the bulk of the civilian welfare expenditures is relatively immune from this budgetary scrutiny.

This material is followed by attempts to indicate several lines of potential improvement in both the preparation of the federal budget in the Executive Branch and the review of the budget by the Congress.

A framework is suggested for preparation of the federal budget which would permit greater choice among the various alternative government programs and a more deliberate and systematic allocation of budget funds among the major purposes of government. Finally, a format is presented of a means of enabling the Congress to relate actions on individual bills and appropriation items to the total budget.

It is hoped that this study will be of value to students of budgeting. To the economy minded, this study describes the problems involved in "cutting" the budget, indicating the more promising approaches and hopefully suggesting certain newer and more effective tools.

For those more concerned with fiscal and economic policy, this study brings to light numerous built-in rigidities in the composition of government spending which inhibit the exercise of discretion in the relating of budget decisions to more general economic or fiscal policy objectives.

To all of these and other groups, this study attempts, by suggesting several approaches, to show the desirability of and need for more effective methods of federal budgeting and programming.

THE PRESSURES FOR GOVERNMENT SPENDING

A STUDY FOCUSED on methods of improving controls over governmental spending necessarily begins with an analysis of the motivations and the pressures that cause the Federal Government to undertake its great variety of activities. These pressures need to be borne in mind in connection with succeeding sections which describe the formal government budgetary process and its built-in rigidities. Official budgetary statistics will be drawn upon, but they will be supplemented by other information.

Fundamentally, the purpose of this section is to show more

clearly the following basic relevant relationships:

> Recipients of federal expenditures are very highly con-
> centrated in specific segments of the population. This
> holds whether the category of analysis used is type of
> expenditure, location of the activity, or the industries
> and groups which are benefited.

> Consequently, the common and usual situation is for any
> given government expenditure program to have a spe-
> cific clientele whose members are benefited more di-
> rectly—or at least so they think—from the particular
> government expenditure program than they would be
> from the relatively modest general tax reduction which
> might be permitted by the elimination of the program.

> These bodies of beneficiaries of expenditure programs
> are motivated to become special pleaders, often on an or-
> ganized basis, for the continuance and expansion of the
> programs in which they are interested.

> The impact of the aggressive and pinpointed support of
> the many programs tends to outweigh, in the absence
> of the rare "taxpayers' uprising," any diffused and
> usually unspoken opposition that may be harbored by the
> general taxpaying public.

In contrast, if the unrealistic situation were to prevail wherein
the direct benefits from each type of government spending were
divided equally among all persons, then the average citizen
might consider himself equally benefited either by a continuation of spending for a given set of government programs or
by a general tax reduction resulting from elimination of such
programs. Under this circumstance, he would be likely to judge
the desirability of private vs. public spending, in the decision area
under consideration, solely from the viewpoint of the national
interest.

Different types of pressures generated in support of the
varied federal expenditure programs are outlined in the expenditure analyses that follow. In the presentation of these
analyses, however, there is no intent to imply that self-interest
pressures generally preclude or necessarily dominate considerations of the national interest in the reaching of decisions on
federal expenditure programs.

Concentration of Expenditures by Function

Opportunities that exist for the build-up of federal expenditure pressures from various segments of the population are readily discernible from simple analyses of the federal budget in terms of agencies by which and functions for which the budgeted funds are expended.

By way of example, Table 1 shows the distribution of federal expenditures for the 1964 fiscal year, as estimated in the budget document when submitted to the Congress, according to the department or agency to which funds are appropriated. It is apparent that a handful of agencies—particularly the Defense, Treasury, Agriculture, and Health-Education-Welfare departments—account for the great bulk of the spending. The aggregate expenditures of these four departments were estimated to represent 73 percent of the total for the year. As demonstrated subsequently, the three civilian departmental budgets contain

Table 1

ESTIMATED FEDERAL EXPENDITURES

BY AGENCY

Fiscal Year 1964

(millions of dollars)

Agency	Administrative budget	Trust funds
Department of Defense	$52,140	$ 32
Treasury Department	11,232	22
Department of Agriculture	6,565	48
Department of Health, Education, and Welfare....	5,742	16,650
Veterans Administration	5,470	548
Funds appropriated to the President [1]	4,375	574
National Aeronautics and Space Administration	4,200	......
Atomic Energy Commission	2,850	......
Department of the Interior	1,165	84
Department of Commerce	895	3,401
Department of Labor	433	3,770
Civil Service Commission	112	1,275
Railroad Retirement Board	12	1,099
All other	3,611	879
Total	$98,802 [2]	$28,382 [2]

[1] Mainly foreign aid.
[2] Totals include $4,707 million in intragovernmental transactions and adjustments.
Source: *The Budget of the United States Government for the Fiscal Year Ending June 30, 1964* (Washington: U. S. Government Printing Office, 1963), pp. 41 ff.

Table 2
FEDERAL GOVERNMENT PAYMENTS TO THE PUBLIC
Fiscal Year 1964

Function	Amount (millions)	Percent
National defense	$56,006	45.7
Health, labor, and welfare	27,424	22.4
Interest	7,723	6.3
Commerce and transportation	6,677	5.5
Veterans benefits and services	5,978	4.9
Agriculture	5,764	4.7
Space research and technology	4,200	3.4
International affairs and finance	2,743	2.2
Natural resources	2,596	2.1
General government	2,197	1.8
Education	1,495	1.2
Housing and community development	1,124	.9
Undistributed adjustments [1]	−1,451	−1.1
Total	$122,477	100.0

[1] Intragovernmental payments that cannot be allocated by functions, such as payments to federal employees' retirement funds. The remainder of the $4,707 of intragovernmental transactions and adjustments (shown in Table 1) has been deducted from individual items.

Source: *The Budget of the United States Government for the Fiscal Year Ending June 30, 1964* (Washington: U. S. Government Printing Office, 1963), p. 430.

large amounts of rigidly established items that are relatively uncontrollable through the appropriating process.

The activities of a number of the agencies included in the "All other" category of Table 1 may have important effects on the nation, but they do not involve large flows of expenditure. The "All other" group includes the Justice, Post Office, and State departments, Legislative Branch, Judiciary, Office of the President and various regulatory commissions, and other independent agencies.

The second of the two standard official classifications of Federal Government spending is in terms of the function, or purpose, for which the disbursements are made. This is presented in Table 2, which also consolidates the administrative budget and trust fund expenditures[1] reported separately in Table 1, elim-

---

[1] The administrative budget covers only funds which are considered to be "government-owned," while trust funds are established to account for funds which are received, held, and expended in a "fiduciary" capacity by the government in carrying out specific purposes and programs. Some of the so-called trust funds involve a questionable fiduciary relationship, particularly as compared to private funds. Cf. Appendix A, p. 86.

inating $4,707 million in intragovernmental transactions and adjustments between the administrative budget and trust funds.

The concentration of federal expenditures in a few program areas is even more apparent in the functional breakdown than was revealed by the distribution of federal expenditures by agency. Two functions—national defense and health-labor-welfare—alone account for 68 percent of the total federal payments to the public.

With the single exception of interest on the public debt, each of the functional categories of estimated expenditures listed in Table 2 has its own clientele of individuals, groups, or other entities that have direct interests in the expenditures and are capable of petitioning for and otherwise seeking to secure the continuance and expansion of the expenditures.

Partial lists of these affected groups, far from complete, are presented here for illustrative purposes:

National Defense: (1) Military personnel, both from the standpoint of their belief in a strong national defense establishment and from the viewpoint of their personal stake in these programs; (2) business and industrial establishments holding defense contracts and subcontracts, and their employees; (3) public and private institutions holding research contracts or receiving research grants, and their personnel.

Health, Labor, and Welfare: (1) The aged, and other recipients and prospective recipients of Old Age, Survivors, and Disability Insurance benefits; (2) persons with pension rights under Civil Service and railroad retirement systems; (3) labor organizations and individual employees with interests in unemployment and related benefits; (4) recipients of public assistance and their families.

Commerce and Transportation: (1) Highway users; (2) highway construction contractors and their employees; (3) commercial aviation and maritime interests receiving federal aid; (4) communities and business concerns receiving Area Redevelopment Administration loans and grants; (5) beneficiaries of Small Business Administration loans.

Veterans Benefits and Services: War veterans and their families.

Agriculture: (1) Farmers; (2) users of Rural Electrification Administration services; (3) rural residents, not necessarily farmers, utilizing credit and related services of the Agriculture Department.

Space Research and Technology: (1) Holders of NASA contracts and their employees; (2) associated scientists.

International Affairs and Finance: Domestic producers of goods and agricultural commodities disposed of through operation of economic aid programs. (Foreign military aid is included under National Defense.)

Natural Resources: (1) Beneficiaries of reclamation and other types of public works projects; (2) sportsmen; (3) conservationists.

General Government: Federal employees (who as a class also have an interest in all other functional categories of federal expenditures).

Education: (1) Colleges and universities benefiting from loans, grants, and research contracts; (2) members of the educational profession and others with particular interests in programs of federal aid for elementary and secondary schools.

Housing and Community Development: Individuals, business concerns, and local governmental units benefiting directly from public housing, urban renewal, and community facility loans and grants.

The above listing illustrates the pattern of the build-up of pressures behind specific expenditure programs.

Regional Concentrations of Federal Expenditures

Certain types of federal expenditures, by their nature, tend toward heavy concentrations in limited numbers of geographical areas. This is true, for example, of expenditures for industrially produced commodities purchased by the Federal Government. Another example is offered by pay and other expenditures that accompany concentrations of military installations and of civilian employees of the government. Similarly, varied types of grants-in-aid, subsidies, and health-labor-welfare payments tend toward regional concentrations, although to a lesser degree.

It follows that where there are concentrations of the expenditures, there also will be concentrations of the "clientele" of the various kinds of federal payments to the public. The result is localization of the pressures for continuance and expansion of federal spending programs.

The extent to which there have developed concentrations of federal expenditures in geographical regions is suggested by estimates prepared recently, by the Legislative Reference Service of the Library of Congress, of the distribution of 1959-61 federal expenditures by resident states of recipients. The word, "suggested," is used because the Library of Congress analysis of state-wide areas necessarily does not deal with the further locali-

Table 3

DISTRIBUTION OF FEDERAL EXPENDITURES BY STATE AVERAGE
PER CAPITA AMOUNTS FOR
FISCAL YEARS 1959-61

State	Per capita average annual amount	Indices	
		Per capita relative to U. S. average (U. S. average = 100)	Amount per $1,000 of personal income relative to U. S. average (U. S. average = 100)
Alaska	$2,629	577	478
District of Columbia	1,547	339	251
Hawaii	1,087	238	241
Maryland	738	162	150
Virginia	705	154	186
Washington	702	154	148
California	639	140	114
Kansas	618	136	145
Rhode Island	617	135	135
Nevada	609	134	106
Wyoming	607	133	128
New Mexico	606	133	161
Massachusetts	594	130	115
Colorado	567	124	120
New Hampshire	556	122	132
Connecticut	540	118	92
Montana	507	111	120
Maine	505	111	131
Arizona	495	109	121
New Jersey	488	107	89
Delaware	484	106	78
Utah	479	105	121
Oklahoma	476	104	125
South Dakota	469	103	133
Texas	454	100	114

State	Per capita average annual amount	Indices	
		Per capita relative to U. S. average (U. S. average = 100)	Amount per $1,000 of personal income relative to U. S. average (U. S. average = 100)
New York	$448	98	78
Florida	446	98	109
Nebraska	435	95	101
Georgia	416	91	127
Illinois	412	90	76
Missouri	412	90	91
North Dakota	406	89	117
South Carolina	403	88	142
Kentucky	392	86	122
Idaho	387	85	103
Alabama	378	83	126
Ohio	370	81	77
Vermont	361	79	95
Pennsylvania	360	79	77
Indiana	351	77	79
Oregon	346	76	75
North Carolina	336	74	106
Mississippi	327	72	136
Arkansas	321	70	117
Louisiana	315	69	94
Iowa	307	67	73
Michigan	306	67	65
Minnesota	304	67	72
Tennessee	302	66	95
Wisconsin	302	66	68
West Virginia	281	62	81

Source: I. M. Labovitz, *Federal Revenues and Expenditures in the Several States, Averages for the Fiscal Years 1959-61* (Washington: Library of Congress, September 19, 1962), pp. 12-15.

zation of concentrations of federal expenditures within the states.

Data based on the Library of Congress estimates are presented in Table 3. In preparing the original estimates, it was found that in the case of such programs as grants to states, social security payments, veterans pensions, and salaries of government employees, the location of the recipient is quite clear. For such items as defense procurement expenditures, the state-by-state distribution was made on the basis of estimates of the location of the employment on defense work. In these and other estimating techniques that were followed, the Library of Congress study is believed to be the most objective analysis of its kind that is available.

In Table 3, the 50 states and the District of Columbia are ranked according to their disproportionate shares of federal expenditures. For example, Texas is shown in the middle of the table with an index number of 100. This signifies that the federal expenditures which were made in or allocable to Texas amounted on a per capita basis to exactly the nation-wide per capita average of the expenditures—that is, to exactly the same amount as if all federal spending were allocated evenly according to population.

In contrast, the expenditures in Alaska were 5.77 times the amount that would have accrued on a nation-wide, even per capita, basis; in Virginia and Washington, they were 54 percent greater. At the other end of the distribution, West Virginia received only 62 percent of the amount that would have obtained on a straight per capita distribution. (It should be borne in mind that these data cover only the fiscal years 1959-61. Presumably, other periods would yield some variations in the individual estimates.)

A related question is the extent to which federal expenditures may be distributed more in accordance with the current wealth of a state (as measured by the flow of personal income) and, hence in some way, in accordance with the taxpaying capability. Table 3 also shows, pertaining to this question, the great variance among states of federal expenditures per each $1,000 of personal income received in the state.

Still another way of looking at the matter of geographical concentrations of federal expenditures is to consider the importance of such expenditures to each state's economy. Figure 1 represents an attempt to do this for defense purchases, which account for approximately 90 percent of federal contracts awarded each year. The 12 states shown with shadings are those in which the direct employment in major defense industries accounts for 10 percent or more of each state's total industrial employment.

In the case of seven states—Kansas, California, Washington, New Mexico, Connecticut, Arizona, and Utah—defense work accounts for 20 to 30 percent of the total manufacturing employment. The Figure is based on data for the aircraft, ordnance, shipbuilding, electronics, and communications industries as representative of defense work. Other portions of the economy, such as steel and metal fabricators, provide supplies and equipment to

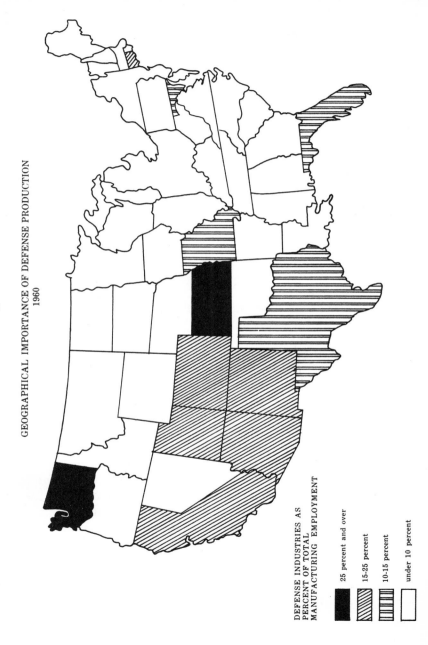

Figure 1

GEOGRAPHICAL IMPORTANCE OF DEFENSE PRODUCTION
1960

DEFENSE INDUSTRIES AS
PERCENT OF TOTAL
MANUFACTURING EMPLOYMENT

25 percent and over

15-25 percent

10-15 percent

under 10 percent

these major defense producers, but are not so heavily dependent on defense production for their sales.

Other states, such as New York, Illinois, and Pennsylvania have absolutely large concentrations of defense industry. However, because of the relative size of their total industrial bases, these latter states do not depend as heavily on defense work as the states designated in Figure 1. In recent years, a number of industrial states have launched intensified efforts to increase their shares of defense production,[2] another indication of the pressures resulting from the uneven distribution of federal expenditures.

Concentration by Industry

Most purchases which the Federal Government makes from private industry are extremely specialized. As revealed by Table 4, more than nine-tenths of the contracts awarded by the Federal Government last year were for military and space equipment. The orders for missiles alone exceeded the purchases of all the civilian departments. In fact, their totals were almost three times the dollar value of orders placed by these other agencies.

It thus becomes apparent that the bulk of federal purchases centers on the output of special types of industrial producers of heavy equipment—aircraft, missiles, electronics, ships, and ordnance. This is not to imply that there is anything insidious in such an industrial concentration. Given the current status of international tensions, the strength of the Communist threat, and the new concepts in military hardware made available through advancing technology, it is to be expected that the bulk of the defense orders should go to industries which have the capability to produce the relatively unique weapon systems and space equipment required for the national security.[3]

---

[2] See, for example, the discussion in the Senate on the Department of Defense Appropriation Bill for the fiscal year 1964, *Congressional Record*, September 24, 1963, pp. 16948-52.

[3] Cf. M. L. Weidenbaum, "The Impact of Military Procurement on American Industry," in J. A. Stockfisch, editor, *Planning and Forecasting in the Defense Industries* (Belmont, Calif.: Wadsworth Publishing Co., 1962), pp. 135-74.

Table 4

CONTRACTS AWARDED BY THE FEDERAL GOVERNMENT

Fiscal Year 1962

	Amount (in millions)	Percent
National Security		
Missiles	$6,690	22.6
Aircraft	5,105	17.3
Electronics systems	3,306	11.2
Ordnance and weapons	2,185	7.4
Ships	1,475	5.0
Construction	1,214	4.1
Space (NASA)	1,054	3.6
All other military	6,173	20.9
Subtotal	$27,201	92.1
Civilian		
General Services Administration [1]	901	3.1
Department of the Interior	328	1.1
Tennessee Valley Authority	214	.7
Department of Commerce	198	.7
All other [2]	718	2.3
Subtotal	$ 2,359	7.9
Total	$29,560	100.0

[1] Includes orders placed by other agencies under indefinite quantity contracts awarded by G.S.A.
[2] Excludes the Atomic Energy Commission, much of whose procurement consists of cost-reimbursed agreements for operation and construction of large-scale facilities.

Source: U. S. Department of Defense, *Military Prime Contracts Awards and Subcontract Payments, July 1961-June 1962*, September 27, 1962, p. 20; U. S. Senate, Select Committee on Small Business, *The Role of Small Business in Government Procurement, 1962-1963*, 1962, pp. 38-39.

Nevertheless, this concentration does mean that the employees of these major government contractors, and the other companies supplying goods and services to the prime contractors as well as to their employees, have become dependent in large measure on government work. Figure 1 illustrates, in part, the resultant geographic distribution of this important economic impact.

Finally, the extent to which some individual industries have come to regard the Federal Government as a major customer may be observed through an examination of the data in Table 5. Here are listed 24 industries for which, according to the latest available Census of Manufactures, the government represents at least one-twentieth of the total market. In several cases, over half of the total sales of an entire industry are made directly to the government.

For individual firms in these industries, the government may represent a far more important source of business than indicated by industry averages. Also the relative importance of the Federal Government as a customer is understated by these data. The table is limited to sales made directly by the manufacturer to the government and does not take account of the portion of the output of these, and other industries, which are purchased by the government through retailers, wholesalers, and other "middlemen."

Some Observations

The preceding analysis has attempted to point out the extent to which individual regions, industries, and groups have become

Table 5
INDUSTRIES FOR WHICH THE FEDERAL GOVERNMENT IS AN IMPORTANT CUSTOMER

Industry	Shipments to Federal Government as percent of total
Complete aircraft	95
Aircraft propellers	75
Engines for aircraft and missiles	54
Shipbuilding and repair	39
Scientific instruments	38
Rice mill products	30
Radio and TV equipment	27
Electrical measuring instruments	15
Trucks and trailers	10
Optical instruments	9
Primary batteries	9
Electronic tubes	8
Photographic equipment	8
Computing machines	7
Internal combustion engines	6
Machine tools	6
Storage batteries	6
Appliance wire and cord	6
Envelopes	6
Misc. general industry machinery	5
Mechanical measuring instruments	5
Wiring devices and supplies	5
Boatbuilding and repair	5
Truck and bus bodies	5

Source: *1958 Census of Manufactures* (latest year available).

attached to or dependent upon specific categories of federal expenditures.[4] These attachments and dependencies may go a long way towards explaining why most effective attempts to reduce requested amounts of federal spending authority have focused on new and proposed programs that have not yet gained a niche in the fabric of society. In any event, it points up the difficulties involved in making major changes in the existing composition and resultant distribution of federal operations and disbursements. This problem is analyzed further, from a different approach, in the next section.

---

[4] Cf. "One of the basic problems of federal finance is the power exercised by organized interest and section groups. . . . Once the federal government embarks on a program of federal aid it is unlikely that it can ever stop or curtail it in the face of these pressures." Joseph P. Harris, "Needed Reforms in the Federal Budget System," *Public Administration Review*, Autumn 1952, pp. 243-44.

FEDERAL SPENDING AND THE LOCALITY

IN CONTRAST to the theme and aggregate approach of the preceding section, this section focuses on a single city to examine the array of governmental activities and funds that are or can be available at the local level. The purpose of this examination is to provide further insight into the character of local pressures which may be generated in support of given federal expenditure programs.

Obviously, a great many cities and towns in the United States contain local representatives of various "old-line" federal departments, bureaus, and agencies, such as the FBI and the Bureau of Labor Statistics. The established operating activities thus represented generally function with only mild efforts to expand in pace with normal population and workload growth.

However, there also are a great many federal programs of a "developmental" character which often are the objects of aggressive local efforts to promote their expansion. There are the programs relating to airports, flood control projects, post office buildings, highways, health research, and similar "investment" type projects for which local communities vie for selection.

The Atlanta, Georgia, metropolitan area presents an interesting case, not because of its uniqueness but because of its typical position as a recipient of and beneficiary from federal programs and activities. It is singled out in this study only because the information is available as the result of a special report by the U. S. Housing and Home Finance Agency.[1] The HHFA lists 33 different federal "developmental" programs, of wide variety, in the Atlanta metropolitan area. The funds authorized for these programs in 1962, including grants as well as direct expenditures and loans as well as loan guarantees, totaled $117,698,000.

Grants and Matching Funds

The Department of Commerce, the Department of Health, Education, and Welfare, the Housing and Home Finance Agency, and the Federal Aviation Agency each provided one or more types of grants and matching funds to the Atlanta area in 1962. These varied from secondary road construction ($5,000) to air pollution research ($35,000). The $35,841,000 in grants to Atlanta could be categorized as follows:

Transportation facilities—primary roads, secondary roads, urban roads, interstate highway, airport construction.

Education—payments to school districts.

Health—hospital construction, waste treatment works, air pollution research, water pollution research, health facility and construction.

Urban facilities—urban renewal, urban planning.

---

[1] Testimony of Robert C. Weaver, Administrator, Housing and Home Finance Agency in U. S. Senate, Committee on Government Operations, *Role of the Federal Government in Metropolitan Areas* (Washington: U. S. Government Printing Office, 1963), pp. 82-83.

Direct Federal Expenditures

In addition to the above grants-in-aid, the Veterans Administration and the Departments of Agriculture, Defense, and Interior each conducted several developmental activities in Atlanta in 1962. These programs were mainly in various fields of natural resource development. The following is a classification of these various direct federal expenditure programs, which totaled $2,296,000 in 1962:

Natural resource development—Altoona Dam recreation facilities, Buford Dam construction, flood prevention, watershed investigation, construction of park facilities, rehabilitation of park facilities, investigation of fish and wildlife, saline water research.

Health—veterans hospital alterations.

Agriculture—farm research.

Defense—construction of reserve, national guard, and other facilities.

Loans and Advances

Loans to individuals, business firms, and local governments in the Atlanta area were also made or planned for in 1962 by the Department of Agriculture, the Housing and Home Finance Agency, the Small Business Administration, and the Veterans Administration. These credit operations (totaling $594,000) came within the following categories:

Urban facilities—direct housing loans, advances for public works planning.

Agriculture—farm loans, rural housing loans.

Business—loans to small business.

Insuring and Leaseback Programs

Finally, three different agencies provided loan insurance and guarantees to the Atlanta area in 1962—the Department of Agriculture, the Veterans Administration, and the Housing and Home Finance Agency. One agency—the Post Office Department

—entered into "leaseback" agreements with private companies for the construction of post offices.

The loan insurance and guarantee programs do not involve any federal expenditure, other than for administration, except in the event of default. Under the "leaseback" program, the Post Office obtains the use of a building constructed to its specifications and makes payments on a lease over an extended period of time rather than paying the full cost of the facility in cash at the outset.

The Federal Government insured or entered into leaseback agreements in Atlanta in 1962 aggregating $78,966,000. The programs may be classified as follows:

> *Urban facilities*—insured housing loans, public housing construction, guaranteed veterans housing loans.
>
> *Agriculture*—insured farm ownership loans.
>
> *Government operations*—post office building leaseback.

Comments

The above description of federal developmental programs in the Atlanta metropolitan area in 1962 shows the great variety of government projects in a single city in a single year. This sample of federal projects yielded programs covering transportation, education, health, urban development, agriculture, and business, as well as defense and government operations.

The federal agencies involved were the Departments of Agriculture, Commerce, Defense, Health, Education, and Welfare, and Post Office, the Federal Aviation Agency, the Housing and Home Finance Agency, the Small Business Administration, and the Veterans Administration.

The financial methods used include grants and matching funds, direct federal expenditures, loan and advance loan programs, and insuring and leaseback programs.

Although the remainder of this study is devoted to the analyzing of federal programs and expenditures from a national viewpoint, it is helpful to keep in mind the significance of the impact of these programs—and the resultant pressures for their continuation and expansion—at the local level. From the view-point of many in the locality, who often rationalize that the government money will be spent anyway, the overriding issue usually is that of whether the locality will obtain its "fair" share. The argument is often voiced that if city "A" turns down the opportunity to obtain a grant from agency "X," the money will go to city "B"—but the relative amounts of federal taxes paid by the people living in A and B will remain unaffected.

THE MECHANICS OF
GOVERNMENT SPENDING

ESSENTIAL TO THE ANALYZING of federal budgetary control problems is an understanding of the mechanics of the spending processes. It is commonly thought that Congress simply enacts appropriations and that the Federal Government agencies then spend the money. In fact, even quite knowledgeable economists sometime short-circuit the process in their descriptions and state that the Congress "legislates government expenditures."

In practice, the process through which Federal Government expenditures are made is a lengthy and intricate one. An attempt is made here to explain the major steps in such detail as may be pertinent to the subject of budgetary control.[1]

Basic Authorizing Legislation

The first step toward establishment of the nature and amount of Federal Government expenditures is not the enactment of appropriations but the making of decisions on the functions which the government should perform. This step normally takes the form of enactment by the Congress of basic legislation creating a given agency, program, or activity and authorizing the appropriation of funds therefore. Some statute, such as the permanent authorization for the Council of Economic Advisers or the annual authorization for the foreign aid program, must be on the books before an appropriation can be enacted to provide funds for the agency or program involved.

Authorizations for limited periods, of course, assure a subsequent legislative review before the program is continued beyond the initial period. For example, the national defense education program, enacted in 1961, was scheduled to expire in 1963 unless extended by additional substantive legislation.[2]

This is the result of congressional procedure rather than statutory requirement. The House rule provides that "no appropriation shall be reported in any general appropriation bill, or be in order as an amendment thereto, for any expenditures not previously authorized by law. . . ."[3] The Senate rule is generally similar.

There are a number of exceptions. For example, the operations of the military establishment have been sanctioned by the Constitution and no general authorizing legislation is necessary; only appropriations enacted by the Congress are needed to enable it to spend government money (except for capital outlays and research and development which do require separate authorizations).

---

[1] A more detailed exposition is contained in M. L. Weidenbaum, "The Economic Impact of the Government Spending Process," *The Business Review,* The University of Houston, Vol. 8, Spring 1961, pp. 3-47.

[2] Public Law 344, 87th Congress, 1st Session, signed October 3, 1961.

[3] *Constitution, Jefferson's Manual and Rules of the House of Representatives,* House Document No. 766, 80th Congress, 2d Session (Washington: U. S. Government Printing Office, 1949), rule 21, clause 2.

In general, authorizing legislation is enacted before funds are granted, and the financial aspects of a government activity are considered separately by the Congress. However, some basic authorizing statutes do simultaneously grant federal agencies financial authority of various types. The Federal-Aid Highway Act, for example, both authorizes the program of aid to the states and enables the Bureau of Public Roads to commit the Federal Government to make specific grants for highway construction.[4] Under this circumstance, the annual appropriation request is for the purpose of "liquidating" the obligations previously incurred and is a mere formality.

In common parlance, this procedure is often referred to as "backdoor spending." Technically, it is backdoor authorization of spending, since the expenditures are made in the same fashion as expenditures out of appropriations and like them, are included in the respective budget totals. As is demonstrated in succeeding sections of this study, however, such "backdoor authorizations" of government spending bypass the detailed review of appropriations committees of both the House of Representatives and the Senate.

Many government corporations and other business-type enterprises, particularly those operating lending programs, are authorized by basic legislation to spend the receipts from their operations without securing annual appropriations from the Congress.[5]

In any budgetary control efforts, consideration must be given to the increment of basic authorizing legislation which is proposed each year—the enactment of new substantive legislation, the extension of expiring legislation, and the modification or repeal of existing statutes—for here is the birth stage, and rebirth and growth stages, of a substantial proportion of federal spending.

This is the stage where the basic policy decisions are made. The kind of farm program, the types of public assistance payments, the level of highway grants are all decided at this stage. However, since the substantive committees of the Congress

---

[4] Public Law 627, 84th Congress.

[5] Budget and Accounting Act of 1921 (U.S.C. 11-16); Budget and Accounting Procedures Act of 1950 (Public Law 784, 81st Congress).

which handle enabling or authorizing legislation (e.g., Judiciary or Foreign Relations or Public Works), rather than the appropriations committees, function during this phase, cost impacts of the new programs ordinarily are relegated to secondary consideration.

The individual substantive committees of the Congress, as they consider legislation with large expenditure significance, usually do not have the opportunity to balance one program against another or to take account of the taxes needed to finance them.[6] The dominant pressure on the legislative or substantive committee ordinarily comes from those favoring a particular program. Prospective beneficiaries, as has been pointed out earlier, are not as concerned with questions of cost as the general taxpayer who advocates economy.

It should be noted that the congressional prohibition on appropriations in the absence of previously enacted authorizing legislation often is a one-way street. In numerous cases, such as the highway program previously mentioned, substantive legislation contains the funding authority which directly—often rigidly—determines the amount of the appropriation that may be enacted.

The reader may sympathize with Dr. Colm's lament concerning the lack of coordination between enabling legislation and appropriations:

> It is a cause for endless bewilderment and wasted effort that enabling legislation often not only establishes the basic purpose of an activity, but also authorizes a specific amount for a specific year.[7]

Requests for New Funds

Each spring, the Bureau of the Budget (a unit in the Executive Office of the President) begins planning the budget for the following fiscal year. With information from each major government department and agency, and subsequent staff work, the

---

[6] "The committees which pass upon authorizations for new or expanded programs have little or no feeling of responsibility for the financial condition of the government. They are primarily interested, as a rule, in advancing the particular program." Harris, *op. cit.,* p. 244.

[7] Gerhard Colm, with the the assistance of Marilyn Young, *The Federal Budget and the National Economy,* National Planning Association, March 1955, p. 30.

President makes an initial determination of the budget level for each major agency. Merely an initial decision at this stage, it will be subject to change at numerous subsequent points in the process.

On the basis of the initial target figures, each department begins detailed preparation of budget submissions. These budgets are not prepared from a clean slate, but take account of the program and expenditure commitments arising from the variety of authorizing legislation which is on the books. Budget preparation generally lasts through the summer and early fall. In the late fall, the Budget Bureau conducts a detailed review of the agency submissions. The outcome goes to the President for his review and then incorporation into the executive budget document.

In January of each year the President transmits to the Congress the budget for the coming fiscal year, the 12-month period beginning the following July 1. In addition to much supporting and historical data, the budget contains the President's estimates of the Federal Government's need for new appropriations and other funding (the various types are described below) for the coming fiscal year. In the case of proposed programs, the President recommends both the needed legislative authority and the necessary "supplemental" appropriation requests which, contingent upon passage of the authorizing legislation, will be sent to the Congress after the consideration of the regular appropriation bills.

From time to time exigencies arise not covered in the budget (such as greater than expected applications for public assistance) which require the President to make further appropriation requests to the Congress. For example, the enactment of legislation with funding requirements not included in the budget or unanticipated U. S. commitments in international conflicts have resulted in such supplemental requests.

Congressional Enactment of Appropriations

The Constitution provides that "no money shall be drawn from the Treasury, but in consequence of appropriations made by law."[8] This constitutional requirement represents the corner-

---

[8] Article 1, section 9(7).

stone of control over federal spending.[9]

From January to June, Congress reviews and modifies the budget and enacts the appropriation bills for the coming year. Often, slippages occur in the congressional schedule and the full backlog of appropriations bills is not worked off until July or August and sometimes much later. In such cases temporary "continuing" appropriations are made.

The budget is not considered by the Congress as a single document nor as one piece of legislation. It is initially referred to the Appropriations Committee of the House of Representatives, where it is separated into parts, each of which is referred to a different subcommittee of the Appropriations Committee. These parts become the basis for the various appropriation bills that pass through Congress. Each subcommittee holds hearings, draws up an appropriation bill, reports it to the full Committee, and the bill proceeds through the normal legislative channels. The House of Representatives, on the basis that all "revenue" bills constitutionally must originate in the lower house, has assumed the initiating prerogative for appropriations as well as tax legislation.

The subcommittees of the Appropriations Committee, both on the House and Senate side, provide the key points of congressional control over appropriations. The Senate group generally acts as a court of appeals for the budget cuts made by the House. It has been quipped that the Senate is the Upper House because it often "ups" the appropriation bills reported by the House of Representatives.

The parent appropriations committees perform a very limited review of the recommendations of their subcommittees.[10] Ordinarily, few items actually are changed during the review of an appropriation bill on the floor of either chamber. Differences

---

[9] For an incisive treatment of the congressional review of budgetary questions, see Robert A. Wallace, *Congressional Control of Federal Spending* (Detroit: Wayne State University Press, 1960).

[10] Professor Smithies states that appropriations bills are considered by the full House Appropriations Committee "for only about an hour or so and they are usually sent unchanged to the floor of the House." Arthur Smithies, *The Budgetary Process in the United States* (New York: McGraw-Hill Book Co., 1955), p. 135.

are reconciled by a conference committee of both bodies. The President normally approves the resultant appropriation bill. Contrary to procedures of some state governments, no item vetoes of appropriation measures are authorized.

Appropriations. The total of fiscal authorizations made available to the federal agencies for a given year is composed of a number of types of enactments. The most prevalent form is the ordinary appropriation, which empowers federal agencies (1) to place orders, enter into contracts, or otherwise commit or "obligate" the government to make expenditures in the future and (2) to make the expenditures required by such obligations.

Appropriations are granted in various forms. "One-year" appropriations, which are the most common form, allow an agency to incur obligations within one fiscal year, the authority expiring at the end of the year. However, obligated balances of such appropriations remain available for two additional years for the making of expenditures. A typical example would be the funds for the General Services Administration.

"Multiple-year" appropriations are available for the incurring of obligations for a specified period of time in excess of one year, with the obligated balances likewise available for two additional years for expenditures. These appropriations may be used for programs of an unusual seasonal nature, such as the Sugar Act program of the Department of Agriculture.

"No-year" appropriations are available for both obligation and expenditure indefinitely. Military procurement and research and development are funded in this manner.

"Current indefinite" appropriations are indefinite in amount. They may be available on a one-year, multiple-year, or no-year basis. The actual amounts involved are determined in specific ways. For instance, the appropriation to the Post Office is based on the difference between postal receipts and authorized obligations.

"Permanent" appropriations are those which become available each year under existing law without new action by the Congress. They may be for definite amounts (such as the annual grant of $50,000 to each state for A&M colleges) or as indefinite as the interest required to be paid on the outstanding public debt.[11]

The last two categories of appropriations are largely immune from effective annual congressional review of the budget recommendations.

Contract Authority. Another type of financial grant is the contract authorization. This empowers the agencies only to incur obligations. In these cases, the agency has to make a later request for an appropriation to pay for or "liquidate" the obligation. Such appropriations are *pro forma* and are usually given only perfunctory review by the Congress. Appropriations to "liquidate contract authorizations" represent authority to make expenditures only, and not to incur additional obligations.

Authorizations to Expend from Debt Receipts. Authorizations to expend from debt receipts usually are used to finance lending and other government enterprises, such as the Commodity Credit Corporation. These authorizations to incur obligations and make expenditures may take the following forms:

(a) Authorization for the Treasury to make public debt receipts available for notes of the government enterprises (since the dollar balances in the bank accounts of the Treasury are not distinguishable by sources, in practice, funds obtained from taxes are lumped together with those from borrowing);

(b) Authorizations for a government enterprise to borrow directly from the public; and

(c) Cancellation of notes previously issued by a government enterprise to the Treasury (the cancellation has the effect of permitting further expenditures to be made by reason of the restoration of previously used authority to borrow from the Treasury).

The obligational authority made available is of the same character as that established by ordinary appropriations. However, authorizations to expend from debt receipts need not go through the appropriations committees nor be included in appropriation bills. Rather, they may be included in substantive legislation

---

[11] For a more technical description of the various types of new obligational authority, see *Budget of the United States Government for the Fiscal Year Ending June 30, 1964* (Washingon: U. S. Government Printing Office, 1963), pp. 126-27 (hereinafter referred to as *1964 Budget*).

reported out by committees handling the particular program and thus be immune from the annual appropriations review.

Re-authorizations. Because of the lags in the federal spending process, there are often requests to extend appropriations and other forms of obligational authority beyond the original period of enactment. The effect of such re-authorizations is the same as if new authorizations were voted in their place. Such re-authorizations generally are not included in the congressional tally of appropriations enacted and, to the extent that they are voted in lieu of new appropriations requested, often are a source of alleged "savings" by the Congress.

New Obligational Authority

The total of appropriations and other financial authorizations made available for a given year is called "new obligational authority" (see Table 6). The bulk of the grants of new obligational authority are ordinary appropriations, but, as noted above, many of them—such as permanent appropriations and authorizations to spend debt receipts—generally by-pass entirely the appropriations committees' annual review. The common characteristic of all these fiscal authorizations is that they empower the agencies to obligate the government to make expenditures in the future.

These authorizations are termed new obligational authority because they exclude the unobligated balances of prior year obligational authority which are still available for current obligation. The total of funds available for obligation, which is of importance for budgetary control, includes both new obligational authority and the unobligated balances.

The granting of new obligational authority (NOA) by the Congress is a major control point over federal spending. Given the grant of new obligational authority, the usual functioning of governmental operations will result in a subsequent flow of expenditures. Hence, to the extent that NOA is embodied in permanent authorizations, that portion of the budget is not subject to current review. To the extent that NOA is enacted by the Congress in indefinite amounts, that portion of the budget is not subject to effective review. Finally, to the extent that NOA is appropriated in non-appropriation bills, that portion of the budget completely bypasses the review by the appropriations committees.

Table 6
TYPES OF NEW OBLIGATIONAL AUTHORITY
Fiscal year 1964
(billions of dollars)

Type	Current authorizations	Permanent authorizations	Total
Appropriations [1]	$96.2	$36.6	$132.8
Reappropriations	*	....	*
Authorizations to expend from dept receipts	.4	.7	1.1
Contract authorizations	*	4.9	4.9
Total [2]	$96.6	$42.2	$138.8

* Less than $50 million.
[1] Excludes appropriations to liquidate contract authorizations totaling $4.5 billion.
[2] Includes administrative budget and trust funds.
Source: *Budget of the United States Government for the Fiscal Year Ending June 30, 1964* (Washington: U. S. Government Printing Office, 1963), p. 39.

Apportionment of Funds

After the Congress has voted funds, the control over spending shifts back to the Executive Branch. The rates at which NOA is obligated are determined by the departments and agencies, subject to the control of the Bureau of the Budget, which is a staff arm of the President's office.

The Budget Bureau apportions to the agencies each quarter the funds appropriated to them. The apportionment power arises from the desire to prevent government agencies from spending their appropriations early in the year and returning for deficiency requests.[12] The apportionment process does not cover the operations of trust funds or certain government-sponsored enterprises.

The apportionment power has been used to keep the amount

---

[12] Executive Order 6166, dated June 10, 1933, gave the Bureau of the Budget the authority for making, waiving, and modifying apportionments. Previously this authority had been vested in the heads of the agencies.

of government spending for a particular item below the full limit of funds granted for it by the Congress. Although the use of apportionments for this purpose is often attacked in the legislative branch and by the potential beneficiaries of the expenditures, such use appears to be sanctioned by law.[13]

Following the making of apportionments, which is a centrally administered form of budgetary control through the Bureau of the Budget, allotments are made by department or agency heads to bureaus or other units within the agencies. Allotments may be made on a monthly or quarterly basis and may limit the use of NOA in terms of objects to be purchased, activities to be performed, or organizational units. Allotments represent an important actual or potential form of internal budgetary control within government agencies.

Incurring Obligations

Within the limits of the apportionment of funds made available to them, the federal agencies place orders, award contracts, hire personnel, and take other similar actions which commit, encumber, or "obligate" their apportioned funds. Except for a few specified instances, the law provides that "no contract for purchase is to be made except under an adequate appropriation."[14] The agencies normally obligate their available funds as rapidly as necessary to carry on their programs, limited mainly by their capability to do so.

To the extent that the goods and services needed by the government are ordered from and produced in the private economy, this is the first stage of the government spending process directly involving private industry. It is also the last step in the process in which the government has complete discretionary control over the timing of its expenditures. From this point forward, the flow of expenditures is influenced by both parties to the transactions, not merely the government.

Making Payments

Because of the multiplicity of steps involved in the federal spending process and the length of time often required by sup-

---

[13] General Appropriation Act, 1951 (64 Stat. 595).
[14] 41 U.S.C. 11; 25 U.S.C. 99.

pliers to produce the goods ordered by the government, there usually is a substantial lag between the time expenditures are authorized and the time they are made.

The lags in the early stages of the process are primarily administrative. It takes time for the agencies to prepare and obtain approval of their apportionment requests, for specifications to be drawn up for individual orders, and for contracts to be awarded. The lag may depend in part on the newness of the program and the necessity for establishing new procedures.

A later and more important lag is technological. It takes time for a contractor to obtain the necessary resources, to draw plans, to negotiate sub-contracts, and to solve technical difficulties. A further delay occurs after performance for delivery, inspection, paper work, and disbursements. There have been instances where payments have been delayed intentionally, particularly to defense contractors, in order to permit the government to stay within the debt ceiling during a period of seasonal pressure.

It was estimated that 52 percent of the NOA requested for the fiscal year 1964 would be spent in that year, with the remainder (except for minor amounts of lapsing appropriations) being spent in future years. Also, only 57 percent of the expenditures in that year would be made out of the authority granted in the year.[15] The remaining expenditures would come out of authority granted in prior years (see Figure 2). This indicates that the time required for effective budgetary control tends to be greater than a single fiscal year.

Reducing Governmental Spending

The actions which can be taken to curtail expenditures generally parallel the actions involved in making expenditures. A reduction in government spending can be initiated at various stages in the spending process. The effects of the actions taken at each stage can be cumulative in their effects on the total of expenditures during any given period.

By the Congress. For example, the Congress may decide to eliminate or reduce the scope of a program by (1) changing its

---

[15] *The Budget in Brief, 1964 Fiscal Year* (Washington: U. S. Government Printing Office, 1963), p. 57.

Figure 2
RELATION OF AUTHORIZATIONS TO EXPENDITURES

1964 Administrative Budget

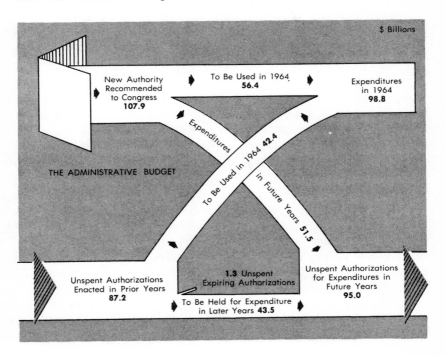

Source: U. S. Bureau of the Budget, *The Budget in Brief, Fiscal Year 1964*, (Washington: U. S. Government Printing Office, 1963), p. 57.

basic statutory authorization or (2) reducing the amount of funds authorized for it during a given period. These actions can be implemented either through eliminations or reductions in the amount of new obligational authority being considered or in the recision of existing obligational authority.

By the President. Independent of congressional action the President may decide, in view of changing circumstances and other developments, that a given agency should not utilize all of its available obligational authority. This decision can be implemented by reducing its quarterly apportionment of funds and placing a portion of the unused appropriation in "reserve."

By the Agencies. The individual agency can reduce the amount spent for a program by slowing down the rate at which it obligates its funds, by obtaining a slowdown in the rate at which particular goods or services contracted for are produced and made available to the agency, or by rescinding contracts and other commitments into which it had previously entered.

Most government contracts provide for their cancellation "in the interests of the government." However, the process of securing reductions in expenditures through cancellation of outstanding contracts has its obstacles. For example, the contractor may claim damages for the unrecoverable costs which he has incurred. Or contract cancellations may create reluctance on the part of business firms to bid on future government work.

In the case of activities such as public works projects, the desire to protect the government investment already made may be decisive in continuing expenditures on a going project in the face of a general effort to curtail goverment spending.

The Points of Control

The preceding explanation of the Federal Government spending process has pointed out the various points of control over the flow of government expenditures. Some of these control points are more effective than others. The key decision points are as follows:

1. *The enactment by the Congress of basic legislation authorizing a given government activity to be performed.* Although not

even part of the formal budgetary process, this step comes closest to being the birth stage of governmental spending. In many cases, such legislation actually contains financial authorizations, by-passing step 3, below.

2. *The review of departmental budget requests by the Bureau of the Budget and the President.* The omission of a proposed expenditure request from the President's budget means that the agency, and its clientele, will generally have an uphill fight in the Congress to add the item to the budget.

3. *The review of appropriation requests by the Congress.* The subcommittees of the House Appropriations Committee (rather than the full committee) are normally the place where the Congress gives the closest scrutiny to the individual items contained in the budget and where the bulk of changes from the President's recommendations are made. The appropriate Senate appropriations subcommittees usually provide a review of the House action. Generally, only a few items in an appropriation bill are considered individually on the floor of either House, and even fewer changes are made at that point. However, the review of appropriation requests by subcommittees and action on them by the House of Representatives and Senate as a whole represent one of the two principal points of effective budgetary control by the Congress. This is the stage at which there is a granting of the bulk of the specific new obligational authority which empowers the government agencies to set in motion a chain of action that ultimately will result in a flow of expenditures.

4. *The apportionment and allotment of funds.* The apportionment power can be and has been used to keep expenditures for a given activity below the level appropriated by the Congress. A similar result, occurring less frequently, can be obtained through the use of the allotment procedure by the head of an executive department or agency. This is the step in the process which most effectively controls the timing of the placement of contracts and the incurring of other obligations to make future expenditures.

5. *The issuance of checks by the Treasury.* Although this is the stage of the process on which public awareness of expenditures is normally focused, it is the least effective of the various points

of budgetary control. Generally, if a commitment has been made and costs incurred, the most that can be done at this stage is to postpone an expenditure. Such action often results in increasing the total cost of an operation. Where the postponement is for the purpose of slowing down the rate of expenditures, then it is an indication of ineffective budgetary control at the earlier stages of the process.

In general this review of steps in the Federal Government spending process points up the fact that if adequate controls are to be exercised over government spending, attention must be given to the early stages where programs and expenditures are authorized, rather than merely to the payments for goods and services already ordered and produced. In a more abstract way, the opportunity for free choice at any given point in time increases as we include more and more of the future within our decision-making. This may be the perennial dilemma of the "budget cutter."

THE BUILT-IN RIGIDITIES IN THE FEDERAL BUDGET

> If a man has a limited budget to spend on cakes and ale, he is likely to be better satisfied if he weighs the advantages of cakes against those of ale than if he allots a fixed sum to cakes and spends what is left for ale.
> —Arthur Smithies

IN THIS SECTION, a proposed federal budget is examined in detail in terms of the leeway for effective controllability under existing statutes and procedures. For this purpose, the budget as originally proposed for the 1964 fiscal year is utilized, since the proposed 1965 fiscal year budget was not available at the time this analysis was developed.

The total amount of new obligational authority (NOA) requested in the 1964 budget came to $138.7 billion. The budget requests of the Department of Health, Education, and Welfare

(HEW to the initiated) which sought total NOA of $23.9 billion, is selected for examination.[1] Subsequently, other departments will be examined with a view toward ascertaining the extent to which built-in rigidities exert strong influence on budget preparation and review.

Department of Health, Education, and Welfare

To provide an understanding of the problems involved, the HEW and other departmental budget requests are examined in terms of meaningful budgetary control categories, rather than by organizational units. The primary purpose is to identify the points at which the various items may be subjected to effective budgetary control—and the points at which they do not respond to review efforts.

As was pointed out earlier, NOA includes permanent and indefinite appropriations that are completely immune to annual review by the appropriations committees. Once established, these accounts do not even appear in the annual appropriations bills enacted by the Congress. Typically, the so-called "trust funds" are financed through these permanent indefinite appropriations.

It develops that HEW lays claim to the lion's share of these permanent indefinite trust funds, including the large social security trust funds as well as some smaller ones. When these automatically appropriated trust funds are deducted from the total HEW request, an interesting relationship emerges:

Line 1.	Total HEW budget request	$23,903,597,000
	Deduct: HEW trust funds	16,746,052,000
Line 2.	Remainder of HEW budget	$ 7,157,545,000

An examination of the remaining $7 billion of the almost $24 billion in the HEW budget reveals that several permanent appropriations also are included. In addition, several appropriation accounts are in the nature of charges fixed by substantive legislation. For example, the $2,950 million for grants to state governments for public assistance payments is established solely by the number of eligible persons who apply for the benefits. The substantive legislation automatically determines the share of

---

[1] The details are contained in *1964 Budget*, pp. 204-21, 311-12; Appendix, pp. 397-486.

state benefit payments which is reimbursed through these grants.

Other fixed charges include the retired pay of commissioned officers of the Public Health Service and the minimum grants of $40,000 per state for library services (see Table 7 for a complete listing).

When these various fixed charges are deducted, the portion of the HEW budget subject to effective budgetary review has shrunk still further:

Line 2.	(from above)	$7,157,545,000
	Deduct: fixed charges	2,975,857,000
Line 3.	Remainder of HEW budget	$4,181,688,000

The various categories of budget requests which are not subject to effective budget scrutiny have not yet been exhausted. Public works construction projects present an especially interesting case. Typically for government agencies with large construction programs, each year's requests are dominated by funds to continue or complete projects begun with funds provided in prior year budgets. The portion of the annual budget devoted to new construction projects is often very small. Hence, the Congress frequently is faced with the alternative of appropriating new funds for construction projects or of suffering the loss of the investment already made. (For example, what is the use of half a bridge?) HEW does not rank high in the roster of federal agencies in terms of its construction programs. However, if account is taken of the portion of the HEW request earmarked for continuation of construction work previously started, the controllable portion of the budget is reduced further:

Line 3.	(from above)	$4,181,688,000
	Deduct: continuing construction	18,007,000
Line 4.	Remainder of HEW budget	$4,163,681,000

Finally, there is a category of budget requests which, although subject to review by the appropriations committees, are not included in the annual appropriations bills. These are the supplementals which often contain the budgetary requests formally submitted, relatively late in the congressional session, after new substantive laws are enacted by the Congress. Although these supplemental requests are considered by the appropriations committees and subcommittees of the Congress, they are not included in the detailed review of an agency's program and activities which the Congress performs in connection with the annual appropriations bills. When these supplementals are deducted, a fairly good estimate of that portion of the HEW budget which is subject to effective budgetary control is obtained:

Line 4. (from above) $4,163,681,000
            Deduct: supplementals   1,619,000,000

Line 5. HEW budget request subject
            to effective review $2,544,681,000

Table 7
DEPARTMENT OF HEALTH, EDUCATION, AND WELFARE
1964 Budget Request
(thousands of dollars)

Trust Funds	
Federal old-age and survivors insurance	$15,568,910
Disability insurance trust fund	1,176,838
Miscellaneous	304
Subtotal, trust funds	$16,746,052
Fixed Charges	
Minimum endowments for A&M colleges	$ 7,650
Minimum grants for library services	2,060
Endowment for A&M colleges (permanent)	2,550
Vocational education grants (permanent)	7,161
Retired pay of commissioned officers (indefinite)	6,436
Grants for public assistance	2,950,000
Subtotal, fixed charges	$ 2,975,857
Continuing Construction Work	
Public Health Service work previously started	$ 13,487
Howard University work previously started	4,520
Subtotal, continuing construction work	$ 18,007
Proposed Legislation	
To be contained in supplemental appropriation bills	$ 1,619,000
Balance	
Budget request subject to effective review	$ 2,544,681
Total new obligational authority	$23,903,597

Dimensions of the cumulative impact of the various items relatively immune to budgetary review thus become apparent (see Table 7). According to these calculations, out of a total HEW budget for the fiscal year 1964 of $23.9 billion, only $2.5 billion, or 11 percent, was subject to effective annual budgetary control by the Congress.

It is true that the Congress may, and often does, reduce through the appropriation process, appropriations requests of the type classified here as non-controllable. For example, the Congress might reduce the requested appropriation for public assistance grants to states, reasoning that the requested figure is larger than required to meet obligations. However, the reductions of the appropriation will not in itself reduce the obligations. If the reduced appropriation later proves to be inadequate, the necessity for a supplemental appropriation will arise and its enactment will be routine.

In order to illustrate other patterns that exist, another agency, the Department of the Interior, is analyzed next. While the bulk of HEW expenditures is devoted to grants to states and social security benefit payments, Interior is primarily concerned with large construction projects and other efforts to develop or conserve the nation's natural resources.

Department of the Interior

Interior's requested NOA for 1964 came to $1,348 million,[2] about one-twentieth of HEW's budget. However, unlike HEW, only a small proportion of this budget request was for trust funds. The $70 million of such trust fund appropriations mainly cover required payments to Indian tribal funds.

Line 1.	Total Interior budget request	$1,348,163,000
	Deduct: trust funds	69,570,000
Line 2.	Remainder of Interior budget	$1,278,593,000

Like HEW, a number of Interior appropriations are of the permanent variety, such as those for claims and treaty obligations. Although these fixed charges are not of the same absolute size as the ones examined previously, they form a significant proportion of the Interior budget request:

---

[2] The details are contained in *1964 Budget*, pp. 221-44, 313; Appendix, pp. 487-576.

Line 2. (from above) $1,278,593,000
         Deduct: fixed charges   263,743,000
                                                ─────────────
Line 3. Remainder of Interior budget $1,014,850,000

Unlike the welfare agency, the Department of the Interior carries on many relatively large construction programs, such as those of the Bureau of Reclamation. The 1964 budget contains requests to continue numerous construction projects of the Reclamation Bureau and the Southwestern Power Administration previously started. When these continuing commitments are taken into account, the Interior budget subject to effective control diminishes sharply:

Line 3. (from above) $1,014,850,000
         Deduct: continuing construction
         work   321,062,000
                                                ─────────────
Line 4. Remainder of Interior budget $693,788,000

Finally, the Interior budget included a relatively small amount for proposed legislation which would be financed through a supplemental appropriation bill, rather than the regular appropriations subject to close congressional scrutiny:

Line 4. (from above) $693,788,000
         Deduct: proposed legislation   25,000,000
                                                ─────────────
Line 5. Interior budget request subject
         to effective review $668,788,000

To recapitulate, out of a total recommended budget for the Department of the Interior of $1.3 billion, only $669 million or 49 percent is subject to effective annual budgetary control by the Congress (see Table 8).

Other Agencies

The Departments of the Interior and Health, Education, and Welfare are by no means atypical in conducting many programs largely immune to budgetary review. The great bulk of the Treasury Department's expenditures, for example, are made under permanent indefinite appropriations to pay the interest due on the national debt.[3] The greater part of the Veterans Administration's budget is devoted to payments of pensions and compensation to eligible veterans. The eligibility is determined by the basic statutes on veterans' benefits and the actual expenditures for a given year depend on the number of qualified veterans who apply for these payments. In years when the Congress initially appropriates too low an amount for this program, subsequent supplemental appropriations are routinely enacted.

Also, 91 percent of the Labor Department's budget is for the permanent indefinite appropriations for the unemployment trust funds. Table 9 shows, for the various major agencies, the limited extent to which their funds are subject to effective congressional budgetary review. The concepts used in preparing these estimates are the same as those used for the Interior and HEW budgets analyzed above. In all borderline and doubtful cases, the programs were classified as controllable.

Table 8
DEPARTMENT OF THE INTERIOR
1964 Budget Request
(thousands of dollars)

Trust Funds	
Indian tribal funds	$ 60,389
Miscellaneous	9,181
Subtotal, trust funds	$ 69,570
Fixed Charges	
Indefinite appropriations of fees and charges	$ 117,766
Public land roads and trails (permanent)	4,000
Claims and treaty obligations (permanent)	161
Other permanent, indefinite, special accounts	137,191
Required lead and zinc subsidies	4,625
Subtotal, fixed charges	$ 263,743
Continuing Construction Work	
Reclamation projects previously started	$ 218,053
Upper Colorado River storage project	99,100
Southwestern power construction	3,909
Subtotal, continuing construction work	$ 321,062
Proposed Legislation	
To be contained in supplemental appropriation bills	$ 25,000
Balance	
Budget request subject to effective review	$ 668,788
Total new obligational authority	$ 1,348,163

[3] For a complete listing of permanent and indefinite appropriations, see U. S. Congress, *Appropriations, Budget Estimates, etc.*, Senate Document No. 162, 87th Congress, 2d Session (Washington: U. S. Government Printing Office, 1962), pp. 678-97, 708-15.

Table 9

SUMMARY ANALYSIS OF 1964 BUDGET REQUESTS
(millions of dollars)

Agency	Requested NOA	Not subject to effective review	Subject to effective review	
			Amount	Percent
Domestic-civilian				
Dept. of Agriculture..	$ 8,195	$ 4,288	$ 3,907	48
Dept of Commerce	4,696	3,715	981	21
Dept. of Health, Education, and Welfare	23,904	21,360.	2,544	11
Dept. of the Interior..	1,348	679	669	49
Dept. of Labor	4,815	4,388	427	9
Treasury Dept.	11,318	10,124	1,194	11
Veterans Administration	6,310	4,755	1,555	25
All Other Agencies....	10,475	5,461	5,014	48
Subtotal	$ 71,061	$54,770	$16,291	23
Security-related				
Dept. of Defense	$ 52,181	$ 2,063	$50,118	96
Dept. of Justice	355	....	355	100
Dept. of State	374	2	372	99
Funds appropriated to the President......	6,154	956	5,198	84
Atomic Energy Commission	2,893	....	2,893	100
National Aeronautics and Space Administration	5,712	....	5,712	100
Subtotal	$ 67,669	$ 3,021	$64,648	96
Grand total	$138,730	$57,791	$80,939	58

Source: *Budget of the United States Government for the Fiscal Year Ending June 30, 1964* (Washington: U. S. Government Printing Office, 1963) and Appendix.

Overall, it is estimated that only 58 percent of requested new spending authority in the 1964 budget was subject to effective review. However, as may be seen in Table 10, there are two different categories of federal agencies involved. Those agencies and departments most closely related to the national security, such as the Department of Defense, NASA, and the AEC, have very few permanent appropriations, trust funds, or other fixed charges. On the average, 96 percent of the expenditure authorizations of these agencies is subject to effective annual control. In striking contrast, only 23 percent of the new spending authority in the other agency budgets—devoted principally to domestic civilian programs—is actually subject to effective review (see Figure 3). The bulk of the expenditures for these civilian-program agencies is authorized virtually automatically as a result of the basic, continuing commitments contained in statutes generally written by and reported out to the floor of the House and Senate by committees of the Congress concerned with the individual program rather than with the state of federal finances.[4]

The foregoing analysis may help to explain the sense of futility on the part of many persons and organizations who have attempted to develop recommendations for comprehensive revisions in the presidential budget recommendations of a given year. The birth stage of much of Federal Government spending, as previously pointed out, is not at the point where appropriations are voted but at the earlier point where the Congress enacts the basic legislative commitment. The most effective point of control is at this earlier stage in the government spending process.[5] Indeed, much of the folklore concerning the uncontrollability of government spending could be eliminated if actions were to be taken on the basis of a proper understanding of the cycle of government spending—which is a far greater period than a single fiscal year. Subsequent sections of this study explore methods of attacking this problem.

Need for Congressional Review of Fixed Budget Items

At this point it is appropriate to ask: "What may be done about the already built-in rigidities of the federal budget?"

Obviously, there are certain naturally uncontrollable items about which little, if anything, may be done. The prime example

---

[4] For an earlier attempt at analyzing the controllability of federal spending, but limited to the administrative budget, see "Controllability of 1952 Budget Expenditures," in Joint Committee on the Economic Report, U. S. Congress, *January 1951 Economic Report of the President* (Washington: U. S. Government Printing Office, 1951), pp. 89-103.

[5] Compare Professor Smithies' statement, "The point to emphasize is that the rates of expenditure are virtually settled by the Veterans' Affairs Committee of the Congress, and its function is to put forward the needs of the veterans rather than to consider the relations of the veterans' program to other programs and to the budget as a whole. The latter function is not performed at all in the Congress." Smithies, *op. cit.*, p. 381.

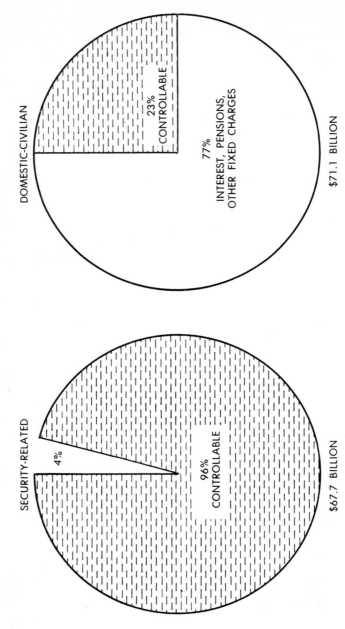

Figure 3

Controllability of 1964 Federal Budget

here is the interest on the public debt which, to express the situation in simple terms, just has to be paid. In this instance, the possibility for reduction lies not in appropriating action or in changes in substantive legislation, but in reduction in the amount of the debt upon which interest is payable.

However, with respect to the bulk of the remaining fixed-cost budget items, there are at least two re-examination approaches which the Executive Branch and/or the Congress, if they were so-minded, might undertake:

1. A survey of all basic laws establishing the fixed obligations in order to identify programs and expenditure items that, through substantive law changes, properly might be converted to an annual budgetary review status.

2. Further examination of fixed-expenditure programs still not susceptible to annual review to determine whether, in the light of the total federal budget problem, certain changes in basic formulas, eligibility rules, or other conditions controlling amounts of expenditures might be desirable.

The objective of a survey of the type described first above would be to seek out permanent expenditure programs wherein conditions have changed to such an extent as to make annual budgetary review the more logical course. A possible example is the program established by section 32 of the Act of August 24, 1935,[6] under which an amount equal to 30 percent of annual customs receipts is automatically appropriated into a permanent, indefinite fund for the "removal of surplus agricultural commodities." These amounts obviously bear little relationship to the "need" for such funds, and recent appropriation acts have authorized transfers of section 32 funds to the school lunch program for the purchase and distribution of agricultural commodities, a program which is itself under annual budgetary review.

Annual grants of $50,000 paid to each state and Puerto Rico for A&M colleges similarly are made under a permanent appropriation act. The Congress has no opportunity to review the annual appropriation request and thus to determine the continued

---

[6] U.S.C. 612c. The portion of these funds allocable to fishery products is transferred to the Department of the Interior to encourage the distribution of U. S. fishery products.

need for or desirability of these payments. There are other examples, such as permanent indefinite appropriations for the Department of the Interior which are tied to a portion of revenues from sales or rentals of government assets and bear little if any relationship to the current requirements for federal expenditures. In this connection, visitor fees at Yellowstone National Park are used automatically to finance educational expenses of dependents of park personnel, while visitor fees at Grand Teton National Park are used for payments to the State of Wyoming, in effect, in lieu of taxes.

Conceivably, many of the statutory requirements of the nature described may have outlived their original purpose of usefulness, and, at a minimum, might be replaced by permissive, authorizing legislation which would require annual congressional action on appropriation requests.

If the second suggested survey were to be carried out, it obviously would constitute a congressional study of major proportions. If set up on a full-scale basis, it would deal with basic laws controlling the operation óf programs such as the highway aid program, social security benefits, veterans' compensation payments, unemployment compensation, numerous kinds of grants-in-aid, and various subsidy programs.

The purpose could be to subject to a coordinated review all of the programs for which the granting of appropriations, because of controlling conditions in basic law, is now a perfunctory and automatic process. In this instance, the controlling conditions would in themselves be the objects of the study.

Such a study would deal with many government programs which, from a political standpoint, are considered to be highly sensitive. Involved would be complications stemming from long-standing jurisdictional perogatives of congressional committees. The undertaking admittedly would be a difficult one.

Nevertheless, the Congress appears to be confronted with the alternatives either of performing periodically such a re-examination of its fixed-cost commitments, or of permitting an already-established 40 percent or more of the fiscal program of the Federal Government to ride along in permanent immunity from effective congressional control.

PROPOSED LEGISLATION: BIRTH STAGE OF GOVERNMENT SPENDING

AS NOTED PREVIOUSLY, the enactment of basic or substantive legislation is the birth stage of new government expenditure programs. Customarily, a variety of such proposals is recommended to the Congress each year. For example, the 1964 fiscal year budget revealed at least 35 identifiable proposals under different budget headings which would commit or authorize expenditures in future years.[1] Additional expenditure proposals, not included in budget submission, always may be effectively initiated from other sources during a congressional session.

---

[1] These items are shown in *1964 Budget*, pp. 7-34, 60-111.

Some of the 35 legislative proposals identified in the 1964 budget have been approved in original or altered form, and others either rejected or allowed to remain pending, during the course of the calendar year 1963 congressional session. However, since the disposition made of individual proposals is not pertinent for purposes of this study, the 35 are hereafter listed and discussed without regard to actions taken on them during 1963.

About one-third of the 35 proposals would have established entirely new government programs, such as the following (1964 NOA request shown in parenthesis where identifiable):

1. A national Academy of Foreign Affairs.
2. Grants to colleges and universities for work in the area of natural resources.
3. Grants to states for water resources planning.
4. Grants to states for planning outdoor recreation and for acquiring recreational lands ($25 million).
5. Federal aid for urban mass transportation ($100 million).
6. Grants for construction of new medical, dental, osteopathic and public health schools and aid to medical and dental students ($34 million).
7. A "long-range" effort to stimulate development of mental health facilities and services.
8. A youth employment program ($100 million).
9. A National Service Corps ("domestic peace corps").
10. A new general education program ($1,215 million).
11. New bureaus of community health and environment health.
12. Health insurance for the aged.

Many of these legislative authorizations would have been permissive rather than mandatory. Nevertheless, if enacted, they could be considered to be moral commitments upon the Congress to fund the respective activities at "good-faith" performance levels. Whatever expenditure levels that might be voted would then be incorporated in the new base line of federal spending.

Many of the 35 legislative proposals reflected in the 1964 budget would have extended expiring programs or increased the authorized size and scope of existing programs. Examples include the following:

1. To increase the rates of military pay ($900 million).
2. To provide additional office and housing facilities for the State Department.
3. To extend the foreign aid program for another year.
4. To eliminate the annual ceiling of $10 million on the budget of the Arms Control and Disarmament Agency ($5 million).
5. To continue the food stamp program ($25 million).
6. To provide further federal acquisitions of land "to protect wilderness areas of great natural beauty."
7. To increase the maximum limits on federal loans and grants under the area redevelopment program.
8. To extend the federal grant-in-aid program for airport construction beyond 1964.
9. To increase the maximum authorization for loans to provide housing for elderly and moderate-income persons.
10. To broaden financial aid to hospitals ($35 million).
11. To increase federal participation in prevention and control of air pollution.
12. To extend assistance to schools in federally affected areas ($254 million).
13. To increase the government contribution and make other changes in the Civil Service Retirement and Disability Fund.
14. To enable the Secretary of Agriculture to stockpile food for civil defense ($30 million).
15. General farm legislation.
16. To shift the farm housing loan program from direct to insured loans ($105 million).
17. To extend the life of the Export-Import Bank for five years.
18. To increase benefits for children and dependent parents of veterans who died as a result of military service.
19. To make permanent "improvements" in the unemployment insurance program.
20. To get the railroad retirement and unemployment insurance systems out of "financial difficulties."
21. To promote maternal and child health ($17 million).

22. To extend the life of the Civil Rights Commission beyond November 30, 1963.

Finally, one of the 35 proposals simply would have exempted an existing program from annual budgetary review. This concerned the Rural Electrification Administration of the Department of Agriculture, which under current rules had been depositing the repayments it received on loans directly into the Federal Treasury. Consequently, new loans have been dependent upon appropriations voted by the Congress. The proposed legislation would have permitted the REA to keep the repayments it received on old loans and use the proceeds to make new loans without further congressional review and approval.

To indicate the fiscal consequences of a "want" list of proposed legislation creating expenditure obligations there is available an old but still useful study prepared by the Bureau of the Budget. This study identifies the portion of expenditure estimates in the 1952 budget, presented to the first session of the 82d Congress, which resulted from legislation enacted by the 80th and 81st Congresses alone. The total came to $7.6 billion of expenditures in an estimated total of $71.6 billion, or more than 10 percent. Eighteen pages of fine print were required to list the various items of new legislation which had been added to the budget during the period covered.[2]

Both the new and old lists of increments to legislative authorizations for government spending programs have a common characteristic in that they would reduce the controllable portion of future budgets. For example, in the case of the first item on the 1964 list—the establishment of a National Academy of Foreign Affairs—the enactment of basic authorizing legislation would at least morally commit future sessions of the Congress to provide funds for such an academy at some minimum level. Another item, the proposed military pay rate increases, would be a relatively fixed charge on the budget, annual congressional discretion being limited to the total payroll cost to be allowed.

Yet from another viewpoint, proposed legislation represents that stage of the overall Federal Government spending process which is most amendable to direct and effective control. At the

---

[2] *January 1951 Economic Report of the President, op. cit.,* pp. 48-67.

outset, the President can refrain from making these new recommendations, or he may modify proposals of administrative agencies to his liking. The Congress can refuse to vote enabling legislation, or modify proposals as its collective judgment dictates. Finally, the President can veto any such legislation that is passed by the Congress.

THE CHOICE AMONG
ALTERNATIVES

Congress never has an opportunity to consider the budget as a whole and weigh the relative needs of all programs. Thus the central purpose of the budget process is largely defeated. —Joseph P. Harris

A GREAT DEAL has been written in the literature on public administration and public finance to the effect that the essence of budgeting is the choice among alternatives.[1] This section is devoted to an empirical attempt at reclassifying budget recommen-

[1] "Budgeting is essentially an economic problem, in solving as it does the allocation of scarce resources among almost insatiable and competing demands," Smithies, *op. cit.*, pp. XIV-XV; ". . . the primary purpose of budgeting ought to be to achieve the most desirable allocation of funds among alternative uses," Edward C. Banfield, "Congress and The Budget: A Planner's Criticism," *American Political Science Review*, December 1949, pp. 1217-18.

dations in a manner to illustrate how practical application may be made of the choice-among-alternatives principle.

Rather than to utilize the existing agency or functional classifications, let us return to first principles. What are the major end purposes for which the various government programs are carried on?

In a world of critical international tensions, the initial purpose that comes to mind is the protection of the nation against external aggressors—to maintain the national security. A variety of programs is suggested, ranging from the equipping and maintaining of our own military establishment and the bolstering of the armed forces of other nations regarded as potential allies, to various types of nonmilitary competition.

A second basic national purpose, one also going back to the Constitution, is the promotion of the public welfare. Here, under the public welfare interpretation that has prevailed, we find the Federal Government operating in the fields of health, pensions, unemployment compensation, relief, and many other such activities.

A third major purpose of government programs has received an increasing amount of attention in recent years—economic development. This area covers the various programs to develop natural resources and transportation, as well as to support education and to attempt to quicken the growth rate of the national economy.

Finally, we have the routine day-to-day operation of the government, such as the functioning of the Congress and the federal courts, the collection of revenues, and the payment of interest on the national debt.

Table 10 shows how the requested funds in the 1964 budget, utilized here for illustrative purposes, were allocated among the four major purposes outlined above. It may come as no surprise that a large portion of the budget—but less than one-half—is devoted to the national security. In contrast, the fact that the great bulk of all non-military spending is devoted to the various welfare programs may not be as widely known. A comparatively small portion is devoted to economic development and, as may be observed, even some of the latter programs may be quite questionable as to their positive effect on the growth and development of the nation.

An examination of the various budgetary documents over the years reveals little systematic attempt to appraise the wisdom or desirability of the overall choice implicitly made in the allocation of government resources among the major alternative uses. It may be mere conjecture to conclude that, possibly, the allocation would have been somewhat different if the appropriation reviews had been approached from this viewpoint. However, added insight to the possible program choices that can be made may be gained from a somewhat deeper analysis of the content of each of these categories.

Table 10

PROGRAM COMPOSITION OF THE 1964 BUDGET
(New Obligational Authority)

Broad Purpose	Amount (millions)	Percent
National security	$ 63,904	46
Public welfare	46,885	34
Economic development	14,296	10
Government operations	13,645	10
Total	$138,730	100

Source: Appendix B, p. 89.

National Security

As would be expected, the bulk of the national security budget was devoted to the U. S. military forces. However, about one-fifth of the total was comprised of programs that would have promoted the national security through somewhat more indirect means, such as non-military forms of competition (NASA and USIA), or bolstering of military capabilities of friendly nations.

The data in Table 11 may be used to indicate the types of "strategic" choices which can be made—or are currently made by default, or accident—in the allocation of funds for national security. First of all, these various programs, in a practical sense, are not now brought together and viewed as a totality anywhere in the congressional review phase of the budgeting process. Hopefully, the approach suggested here would lend itself to first raising and then answering questions such as the following:

Would the national security be improved by shifting some or all of the $12 billion for foreign aid and non-military competition to the U. S. military establishment itself?

Table 11
NATIONAL SECURITY PROGRAMS
1964 Budget

Program category	Amount (millions)	Percent
U. S. military forces	$51,473	80.6
Scientific competition (NASA)	5,712	9.0
Foreign non-military aid	4,689	7.3
Foreign military forces	1,480	2.3
U. S. passive defense	318	.5
Political and psychological competition (USIA)	217	.3
Arms control and disarmament	15	*
Total	$63,904	100.0

* Less than .05 percent.

Conversely, would the national security be strengthened by moving a proportionately small share of the direct military budget, say $500 million, to USIA or the arms control effort, thus to produce proportionately large increases in these latter programs?

Are we putting too much into foreign economic aid and not enough into the Voice of America (USIA)? Or vice versa?

Would we be better off if we shifted the funds now going to passive (civil) defense to the U. S. Arms Control and Disarmament Agency? Or vice versa?

Utilization of the type of approach suggested here may lead not only to attempts to answer questions such as these but, more fundamentally, to widen the horizons of budget reviewers.

Public Welfare

As shown in Table 10, about one-third of requested new obligational authority in the 1964 budget was devoted to programs in the general area of the public welfare. Although the reader may wish to challenge, or change, the classification of some of these items, the tabulation of public welfare programs in Table 12 illustrates the assortment of choices that are made as to uses to which public funds are to be put.

The several social insurance and retirement programs receive the bulk of the funds for public welfare. However, this is hardly a conscious decision. As pointed out earlier, the expenditures for these programs—such as the old-age and survivors insurance systems—are determined by basic statute and generally are not even reviewable during the appropriations process. For this and other reasons, it should not be surprising that they have grown to dominate the nondefense budget, with their commitments exceeding by a wide margin the total for the various economic development programs (see Table 13, below).

Likewise, the commitments under the various agricultural price support programs (in the category of "assistance to farmers and rural areas") exceed all of the programs of urban housing and facilities. Again, the farm subsidy program is generally set by substantive law, rather than through annual appropriations.

This level of detail also permits some cross-comparisons of government programs between the "national security" and "public welfare" categories. For example, the $7.2 billion for aid to farmers is roughly equal to the total allocated for civilian space exploration ($5.7 billion) plus foreign military assistance ($1.5 billion). Would some trade-off between the public welfare and national security areas result in a net advantage? Again, we are trying to answer the question, "Would an extra dollar (a billion, in the case of the government) be more wisely spent for program A or for program B?" This is the fundamental question implicit in the allocation of budgetary funds or any other resources. The literally thousands of pages of budget justifications and congressional hearings which are published each year fail to show even any awareness of the problem, much less any attempt at an answer.

Yet, it is suggested that the approach described here would be useful in attempting to achieve various basic aims through the budgetary process. For one thing, an attempt to balance the outgo side against projected revenues might be more successfully accomplished than in the past through this process of weighing alternative programs against each other and choosing the more useful or higher priority items. Similarly, during an inflationary period, increases in federal revenues might be consciously allocated between say, greater welfare and faster economic growth—or even might be utilized for debt retirement—

rather than to be used up through an unplanned addition of unrelated individual appropriations.

Table 12
PUBLIC WELFARE PROGRAMS
1964 Budget

Program category	Amount (millions)	Percent
Social insurance and retirement	$22,314	47.6
Aid to farmers and rural areas	7,290	15.5
Public assistance	4,919	10.5
Unemployment insurance	4,407	9.4
Health	3,084	6.6
Veterans compensation	2,061	4.4
Urban housing and facilities	1,667	3.6
Other welfare	1,143	2.4
Total	$46,885	100.0

Economic Development

In the exploratory categorization of government programs
presented here, various activities are listed under the heading
"Economic Development" (see Table 13). Judgments may differ,
of course, as to whether certain of the programs involved here
actually contribute to the more rapid growth and development of
the American economy. The very existence of sharp judgment
differences, however, emphasizes the need for better means of
evaluating the worth of the respective programs.

A brief examination of the composition of the economic development category may be revealing. Transportation facilities
account for the largest single share and, when combined with
natural resource programs, account for fully two-thirds of the
total.

Table 13
ECONOMIC DEVELOPMENT PROGRAMS
1964 Budget

Program category	Amount (millions)	Percent
Transportation facilities	$ 5,066	35.5
Natural resources	4,484	31.4
Education and general research	2,839	19.8
Aids and subsidies to business	1,743	12.2
Economic regulation	164	1.1
Total	$14,296	100.0

A further breakdown also indicates another level of trade-offs which is possible. The amount shown for transportation facilities consists of three types of programs, as follows (in millions) :

Land transportation	$3,892
Air transportation	810
Water transportation	364
Total	$5,066

The dominance of land transportation, mainly the federal-aid highway program, is striking. It accounts for over 76 percent of the transportation total. Would a revised trade-off between land and air transport expenditures be advisable? Between land transportation ($3.9 billion) and education and general research ($2.8 billion)? Raising these questions should not be taken as expressing value judgments, but rather as indicating a pattern for decision-making.

As indicated previously, some programs included under the economic development category may be questionable as to their economic benefits. In the case of natural resource programs, the bulk of the funds is devoted to the dams, power, and related multi-purpose projects of the Corps of Engineers and the Bureau of Reclamation. Yet many authorities question the merits of individual projects.

Professor Otto Eckstein of Harvard University concluded in a study published by the congressional Joint Economic Committee in 1957:

> In the case of at least half of all the projects that are being built, it is unlikely that their effect on national income will be positive. . . . The return on many projects is so low that their net effect will be to reduce the rate of growth of the economy.[2]

Professor Eckstein pointed out that the techniques used by federal agencies to measure benefits from water resource projects "considerably overstate the additions to national income" by inflating the indirect or secondary benefits which might accrue from the expenditure.[3] However, a more basic shortcoming of

---

[2] Otto Eckstein, "Evaluation of Federal Expenditures for Water Resource Projects," in Joint Economic Committee, U. S. Congress, *Federal Expenditure Policy for Economic Growth and Stability* (Washington: U. S. Government Printing Office, 1957), p. 667.

[3] *Ibid.*, pp. 658-59.

these projects may be the contribution they make to the large farm surpluses—accomplished through the expanding of the land areas on which farm products, not needed to meet consumer demands at current prices, are being grown.

Here there appears the possibility of an unusual agricultural-resource trade-off in which, to some extent, a reduction in funds for natural resources would permit a reduction in farm subsidy outlays. This illustrates another aspect of the broadening of the vista of budgetary review. Not only can we examine choices among programs, but we can also examine the consistency of the various programs in relation to each other.

Government Operations

The final category of government programs represents, as best may be estimated, the general costs of operating the government in its routine, day-to-day functions. Table 14 shows that approximately three-fourths of the funds in this category covered the permanent indefinite appropriation for the payment of interest on the public debt. The bulk of the remaining one-fourth of the outlays for government operations was devoted to collection of internal revenue and the housekeeping functions of the General Services Administration, such as the Public Buildings Service and the Federal Supply Service.

Table 14

GOVERNMENT OPERATIONS
1964 Budget

Program category	Amount (millions)	Percent
Interest payments	$10,103	74.1
Housekeeping functions	2,578	18.8
Judicial and law enforcement	430	3.2
Conducting foreign relations	411	3.0
Legislative functions	123	.9
Total	$13,645	100.0

Utilization of the Purpose Approach

To some extent, the material in this section properly may be criticized as being essentially "just another functional classification of budget programs." This would miss the point. The present functional classification used in the federal budget (see Table 2) is merely a reporting device and not a mechanism for decision-making in the actual budgetary process. The Congress is well aware of this situation and, except as to the rough paralleling of government functions and appropriation subcommittee assignments in a very gross manner, largely avoids the functional classifications.

The theme of this section, in contrast, is that the budgetary process itself should make use of a program or purpose approach to decision-making. To some extent, in response to recommendations of various Hoover Commission reports [4] and others, a purpose approach to federal budgeting has been utilized in recent years. However, it has been used solely to review detailed activities comprising a single appropriation account (e.g., civil actions versus criminal actions in the Department of Justice's legal staff). It is suggested here that the purpose approach be broadened to cover basic functions and purposes for which the detailed government activities have been instituted in the first place (see Appendix B, p. 89 for program composition of the 1964 budget).

This may be an instance where the public may respond to a proper presentation of the alternatives. A recent detailed study of public attitudes toward government spending programs indicated that a clear majority of the sample of persons interviewed believed increases in one area of government spending should be offset by commensurate decreases in other areas, rather than being additive.

The following specific question was posed: "If the cold war with Russia should cost us more money during the next few years, do you think the government should raise taxes or spend less on other things, or go further into debt?"

Approximately 62 percent of the sample preferred spending less on other government programs, rather than either increases in taxes (29 percent) or deficit financing (4 percent). Also, some were uncertain or otherwise qualified their views.[5]

---

[4] U. S. Commission of Organization of the Executive Branch of the Government, *Budgeting and Accounting* (Washington: U. S. Government Printing Office, 1949), pp. 7-17, 77-84.

[5] Eva Mueller, "Public Attitudes Toward Fiscal Programs," *Quarterly Journal of Economics*, May 1963, p. 218.

During the last few years, there has been one very good example of congressional interest and concern with a functional or purpose approach to budgeting. In the case of the Department of Defense, the Executive Branch has made the basic budget decisions via such an end-purpose approach.

Although military appropriation requests still are submitted on the basis of operations and maintenance, personnel, procurement, and similar classifications, the underlying decisions are made on a program basis. Here it is a question, for example, of strategic versus limited war capability—or offensive versus defensive forces. Within such overall categories, the alternative weapon systems which could fulfill the same end mission are compared with each other.[6] One case would be the Navy's Polaris missile system competing with the Air Force's Minuteman ICBM for strategic funds without regard to the necessary crossing of the organizational lines of the two services. (In earlier years it was more a case of the Navy's strategic missiles competing with Marine Corps ordnance—two relatively unrelated items—within the Naval procurement budget.)

The advantage of this new method of budget presentation is that it permits direct comparison of the various programs of the different services which are close substitutes for each other or which contribute to a common mission or purpose. Clearly, this is a general methodology which has application in budgeting for nonmilitary programs.

Recent military appropriations and authorization hearings and reports show increased congressional attention to the new program approach to military budgeting. This may not be surprising in view of the fact that the Secretary of Defense uses this approach in presenting his major recommendations and supporting analyses.

It may be reasonable to assume that the incorporation in the Budget Message and the Budget Document of the approach here suggested might result in growing congressional and public interest. Alternatively, a congressional committee staff could re-

---

[6] Cf. David Novick, "Planning Ahead in the Department of Defense," *California Management Review*, Summer 1963, pp. 35-42. Mr. Novick's initial treatment of this subject is contained in Rand Corporation Report 254, *Efficiency and Economy in Government Through New Budgeting and Accounting Procedures*, February 1, 1954.

work the existing budget submissions within this framework for review, say, by the entire appropriations committees prior to their detailed review of individual appropriation requests. This might permit the parent appropriations committees to set general guidelines and ground rules for detailed budgetary review. This would be quite different from the present situation where the overall allocation of budgetary funds among the major functions of government is more nearly the accidental result of a myriad of individual budget decisions.

Hopefully, this suggested procedure might permit the Congress to exercise the role in budgetary review envisioned by Professor Harris:

> . . . instead of attempting to decide whether an activity could be carried on as well with fewer employees or less expenditures for supplies, automobiles, postage, or public relations, it should give more attention to whether the program is needed at all, or whether the money could be better spent for something else.[7]

The Choice of Not to Spend

Up to this point, the exploratory treatment of the subject of budgetary alternatives has been limited chiefly to examinations of trade-offs in expenditures among programs, based upon evaluations of the worth of end purposes to be served. This emphasis on choices among programs has been for the purpose of explanation and illustration of the principle involved, but the treatment given to the subject is not intended to imply that another kind of choice is not available.

The basic choice in any budgetary decision, obviously, is whether funds that would be required for a given purpose should be spent at all. Would the national welfare be benefited more by an increase in private spending (perhaps fostered by a reduction in tax rates) than by an increment in governmental expenditures?

---

[7] Harris, *op. cit.*

THE SEARCH FOR IMPROVEMENTS
IN BUDGET-CONTROL TECHNIQUES

At a certain village in La Mancha, which I shall not name, there liv'd not long ago one of those old-fashion'd gentlemen who are never without a Lance Upon a Rock, an old Target, a lean Horse, and a Greyhound.
—Miguel de Cervantes

IN THE COURSE of consideration of both the expenditure and revenue aspects of the 1964 fiscal year budget, and in preparatory steps looking toward a new budget year, there has been a marked intensification of attention to the question of federal expenditure control.

Should the Congress determine to undertake a serious, intensified search for improvements in budget-control techniques, it will be able to take advantage of much exploration in the past toward this objective.

Over the years, numerous proposals have been made for improvement of congressional review of the federal budget. Suggestions along these lines have been made by both advocates of greater economy and proponents of new or expanded government spending programs.

It is true that despite the variety of the proposals there has been, since the enactment of the historic Budget and Accounting Act of 1921, only slight modifications of the way in which the Congress acts on the budget.

The fact remains, as shown in this study, that serious weaknesses exist in the means at the command of the Congress to exercise effective budgetary control on a coordinated basis and in accordance with the basic purposes of budgeting. The need is for improvements that will better equip the Congress (1) to make budget-oriented judgments at the authorization, or birth-stage level of expenditure programs, (2) to arrive at an evaluation of individual expenditures from a total-budget viewpoint, and (3) to utilize knowledgeably the opportunity through the budgeting process to choose among the various purposes for which given amounts of funds can be spent.

Organization for Budgetary Control

Of the many suggestions for budgeting improvements that have been made over the years, the great majority consists of proposals to change the congressional organization for budgetary control. Emerson Schmidt has stated that "one of the major difficulties to sound Congressional control over budget matters stems from the manner in which its committee structure is organized." [1]

The basic work of the Congress, of course, is conducted through its committees and subcommittees. As discussed earlier, most of the congressional committees participate in some stage of the budgetary review process, either in the authorization or the funding of individual programs. The entire gamut of budgetary actions taken by the Congress is conducted in a fragmented fashion, even though the budget—at least the formal budget document—comes to the Congress as a unit.

---

[1] Emerson P. Schmidt, *Economic Analysis of the Budget* (Washington: Chamber of Commerce of the United States, 1963), p. 38.

The Legislation Reorganization Act of 1946 made an unsuccessful effort to improve congressional control of the budget. Section 138 of the Act created a joint committee composed of all members of the four taxation and appropriation committees of the two chambers of the Congress. It also directed that the committee (a) compare the estimated total receipts and the total expenditures proposed in the budget for the coming year, and (b) recommend a ceiling on total expenditures to serve as a control of the total amount of appropriations.

Although a noteworthy attempt, section 138 proved unworkable in the 80th and succeeding Congresses. This failure was largely attributed to the cumbersome committee setup involved and to the lack of necessary staff.[2]

Many of the more recent suggestions for changes also are in terms of establishing a new congressional committee. A joint committee on the budget or on fiscal policy has often been advocated in order to give overall consideration to revenues, appropriations, expenditures, and debt management by the Congress as a whole. It has been suggested that ranking members or representatives of the Ways and Means and Appropriations committees of the House of Representatives and the Finance and Appropriations committees of the Senate could meet as one joint committee to consider the overall aspects of the revenue and expenditure programs.

During each of the last five Congresses, the Senate has passed, frequently by unanimous consent, a bill to create a joint House-Senate Committee on the Budget (e.g., S. 537, 88th Congress). Such a committee would act as a service committee, similar to the Joint Committee on Internal Revenue Taxation on the revenue side, to aid the appropriations committees in a more systematic and detailed review of budgetary issues.[3]

Other specific legislative proposals introduced in prior Congresses to change the organization or structure of the Congress

---

[2] A more detailed discussion of the organizational aspects of congressional review of the budget will be discussed in a forthcoming AEI study by Professor John S. Saloma.

[3] U. S. Senate, Committee on Government Operations, *Create a Joint Committee on the Budget*, Hearings on S. 537, March 19 and 30, 1963; *Joint Committee on the Budget*, Senate Report No. 141, 88th Congress, 1st Session.

and of congressional units in order to improve budgetary review have included the following:

1. A joint congressional committee to audit all government agencies (Senate Joint Resolution 42, 80th Congress).

2. A Legislative Bureau of Audit and Review (Senate Bill 3482, 82d Congress).

3. A Committee on Fiscal Planning for the House of Representatives (House Resolution 481, 86th Congress).

4. A select committee to study the fiscal and budget organization and operations of the Congress.[4]

The above suggestions appear to have some merit and, if adopted, might contribute to improved congressional controls over government spending. However, either or both Houses of the Congress have consistently opposed these and similar proposals.

The proposed joint Senate-House committees generally have been turned down in the House of Representatives, which is strongly concerned with maintaining its primacy on financial matters. The constitutional mandate that all revenue bills must originate in the House has been interpreted to cover also bills to appropriate the revenues, although there may be some arguments to the contrary.[5] Attempts to establish new committees in either House also have been interpreted as being dilutions of the powers and responsibilities of the respective appropriations committee and, hence, have been unsuccessful.

It appears to the writer that future attempts to improve congressional budgetary control must take into account these fundamental jurisdictional considerations.

Congressional Procedures

Another "family" of suggested improvements covers omnibus appropriation bills, special sessions, joint hearings, and similar

---

[4] Cf. U. S. Senate Committee on Government Operations, *Financial Management in the Federal Government*, Senate Document No. 11, 87th Congress, 1st Session, pp. 221-31, 363-69.

[5] "Authority of the Senate to Originate Appropriation Bills," staff memorandum reprinted in U. S. Senate, Committee on Government Operations, *Create a Joint Committee on the Budget*, Hearings, *op. cit.*, pp. 81-114.

procedural changes. Although not involving changes in congressional committee structure, these proposals do require significant departures from either the way in which the Congress meets to consider the budget or in the nature of appropriation legislation.

For example, in 1949 the Senate adopted a resolution (Senate Report 616) requiring the incorporation of the traditionally separate appropriation measures into a one-package or omnibus appropriation bill. This obviously was an attempt to have the Congress act from a total-budget viewpoint. At the insistence of its Appropriations Committee that existing authority was adequate, the House of Representatives declined to report a bill to authorize this change.

The House Appropriations Committee did voluntarily adopt the procedure recommended by the Senate for the fiscal year 1951. However, because of dissatisfaction compounded by the additional requirements of the Korean War, the House Committee subsequently voted to return to the old procedure of reporting separate appropriation bills for the following years.

Specific objections to the omnibus measure included that of the delay caused in passage of appropriations, due to the fact that the Senate would have been prevented from starting work on the many appropriation items until all of them were approved by the House. Also, the omnibus bill lent itself to the addition of legislative riders. As a practical matter, the President could not have vetoed such riders which he deemed objectionable unless he were willing to veto the whole omnibus bill and delay (except for temporary continuing appropriations) the financing of all government agencies.

Other procedural suggestions have been for the appropriations committees of both Houses to hold joint hearings on the appropriation bills; for a regular annual budget session of the Congress to be held separately from the session on other legislative matters (Senate Bill 2846, 85th Congress), and for the Congress to stay in session until it balances the budget (Senate Joint Resolution 126, 84th Congress).

These various attempts to change congressional procedures have failed to obtain even the level of support gained by some of the proposals to establish new committees.

Suggested Mechanism to Assist in Budget Review

In the absence of reform of a more basic character—and with the thought of encouraging such reform—the writer suggests here a budget reviewing mechanism, representing an approach somewhat different from the previously reviewed proposals. It would not require changes in the organizational structure of the Congress or alterations in legislative-executive relationships. Rather, the suggestion is in terms of an analytical mechanism which can be used by the existing committees of the Congress.

The suggested mechanism, it is believed, would assist in overcoming the serious shortcoming in the congressional review of the budget that springs from lack of a workable means of reviewing an individual revenue or expenditure decision in the light of the total budget picture. It also should be helpful in the matter of alternative choices by the Congress in attacking the budget problem.

A Budgetary Scorecard. Table 15 presents the framework of this suggested tool of budgetary review. In the form of a "Budgetary Scorecard," it is intended to be a very simple, straightforward application of economic analysis to pertinent budget facts. In essence, its purpose would be to show the effect of individual budget decisions (i.e., viewing each case as the marginal case) on the overall state of federal finances.[6]

The budgetary scorecard would be far less ambitious than the earlier proposals reviewed here. It merely would be intended to serve as an informational aid to the various congressional committees that act on authorizing or appropriating legislation. It is put forward in the hope that it might constitute a small, initial step towards increasing more effective congressional control over government spending.

Except for using the 1964 budget estimates for the "submission" columns for the fiscal years 1963 and 1964, the scorecard contains hypothetical data for illustration only.

---

[6] Cf. Professor Paul McCracken's statement, "Whatever the details of the solution may be, this absence of any explicit Congressional consideration of total expenditures remains in principle an important gap in budgetary procedures." "Budgetary Concepts: A Symposium," *Review of Economics and Statistics*, May 1963, p. 147.

Table 15

ILLUSTRATIVE BUDGETARY SCORECARD
(On Basis of Cash Receipts from and Payments to Public)

	1963 (Current Year) Submission	1963 (Current Year) Revision	1964 (Budget Year) Submission	1964 (Budget Year) Revision	1965 (Future Effect) Estimate	1965 (Future Effect) Revision
Budget Totals (billions of dollars):						
Receipts	$108.4	$108.0	$112.2	$112.5	$116.0	$115.0
Expenditures	116.8	116.0	122.5	124.0	125.0	128.0
Deficit (or surplus)	$—8.3	$—8.0	$—10.3	$—11.5	$—9.0	$—13.0
Item Under Consideration:						
To Extend Assistance to Schools in Federally Affected Areas (millions of dollars)						
Allowance contained in above estimates: Expenditures (NOA)	......	......	148 (254)	165 (270)	250 (260)	265 (280)
Amount being considered: Expenditures (NOA)	......	......	......	200 (300)	......	300 (350)
INCREASE (or decrease) in budget deficit	......	......	......	+35	......	+35

Several assumptions have been made in "filling out" the score-card:

(1) That some congressional committee or staff (to be dis-cussed below) has supplied (a) the revisions for 1963 and 1964 in the light of congressional action since the original submission of the 1964 budget and (b) the data for the following year (1965, in this case), to provide some indication of the future or "full year" effect of the current congressional decisions.

(2) That the estimated deficit for the budget year (1964) has been increased through more liberal congressional action on previous items.

(3) Regarding the specific item under consideration, that pressures are evident to increase the existing program of aid to schools in areas heavily affected by federal activities because of the deferral of the President's proposal for a broad program of general aid to education.

Hopefully, the type of information in Table 15 would show the congressional committee that (1) the prospective deficit for 1964 is larger than 1963, (2) congressional action to date has increased the prospective deficit further, and (3) the specific item under consideration, if enacted at the currently recommended level, would raise the budget deficit further still.

It is problematical whether such data would, in fact, have any influence upon the deliberations of individual committees. It would, however, provide a simple technique and substantiating figures for specific members of these committees who desired analytical support for their positions.

As the scorecard might be used in conjunction with actions on a variety of expenditure authorization, appropriation, and reve-nue bills, it would maintain constantly for the attention of the Congress a recording of the ebb and flow of the current status of the budget picture for the ensuing fiscal year (or current year after the July 1 milestone in a congressional session). The trend of congressional actions toward a larger or smaller deficit, or a balanced budget or surplus status would be clearly revealed.

At the same time, use of the scorecard would be a means of appraising in concrete terms the effects of each individual fiscal action on the total budget outcome.

Implementation of Scorecard Procedure. Use of the score-card idea would require services of staff personnel of congressional committees or administrative agencies, to do the "book-keeping" and to develop estimates of effects on expenditure or revenue figures of individual actions changing proposed new obligational authorization or affecting anticipated revenues. Also, the device could be expanded if congressional committees dealing with substantive legislation would undertake, to a greater degree than has been the case in the past, to elicit from proponents of new expenditure programs their best estimates (with supporting data) of anticipated expenditures under the program for at least a five-year period into the future.

A number of decisions would need to be made on matters of implementation. For one thing, the initial estimates of total receipts and expenditures either could be taken directly from the presidential recommendations or could be subject to change by a congressional committee (such as by substituting the revenue estimates prepared by the staff of the Joint Committee on Internal Revenue Taxation).

Also, the choice of budget concept would have to be made, such as between the administrative budget or the statement of cash receipts from and payments to the public. Because of the more comprehensive coverage of the latter, it has been used in Table 15.[7]

As previously indicated, the current reporting of budgetary action envisioned in the proposed "scorecard" would not be limited to pending actions by the appropriations committees but would also be utilized by the substantive committees considering basic legislation. Hence, the birthstage of government spending programs, now often relatively immune from budgetary considerations, would be exposed to the type of financial concern currently shared only by the appropriations and tax-writing committees.

The scorecard would also constitute a first step attempt to extend the time horizon of federal budgeting. Estimates of fu-

---

[7] The alternative budget concepts are discussed below. For a clear and straightforward explanation of the desirability of such a comprehensive cash concept, see Chamber of Commerce of the United States, *Improving the Federal Budget*, report of a special committee established at the request of President Kennedy, 1962.

ture year expenditure impacts of new programs would not be binding but they would at least apprise the Congress of spending plans anticipated for the future.

This type of information on future impacts could be especially useful in connection with reviews of proposed new programs where the initial requirements appear to be small, but the total eventual cost may substantially exceed the value of benefits to be derived. The Senate Subcommittee on National Policy Machinery has colorfully stated that "a 12-month budget reveals only the top of the fiscal iceberg." [8]

The scorecard could be maintained by the staffs, possibly augmented, of the appropriations committees of each chamber. Alternatively, the task could be assigned to a Joint Committee on the Budget should the Congress decide to establish one. Another possibility would be to develop the capabilities of the General Accounting Office, which is a congressional rather than executive agency. The staff involved would need to keep abreast of the actions of the various substantive committees which provide financial authorization for future federal spending. Also, the working relationships would have to be developed so that the scorecards, when properly prepared and made available, would actually be utilized in the deliberations of these various committees.

During the past year, a very short "score-keeping" step has been taken through progress reports on appropriation legislation inserted by the chairman of the House Appropriations Committee in the *Congressional Record*.[9] Representative Cannon included a summary of the action which had been taken on the appropriation bills during the current congressional session, together with an approximation of the portions of the President's budget which were yet to come before the House of Representatives for consideration.

However, Mr. Cannon's summary excluded, by its very nature, the various permanent appropriations as well as "backdoor" spending authorizations which are reported by the substantive committees rather than being included in the appropriations leg-

---

[8] U. S. Senate, Committee on Government Operations, Subcommittee on National Policy Machinery, *The Bureau of the Budget and the Budgetary Process* (Washington: U. S. Government Printing Office, 1961), p. 4.

[9] Cf. June 17, 1963, pp. 10305-07.

islation. Also, the congressional report is on the basis of appropriations (including the *pro forma* appropriations to liquidate contract authorizations) rather than the more comprehensive "new obligational authority" concept used in the budget. By its very nature, Representative Cannon's report is based on the conventional budget concept, rather than the more embrasive cash approach used in Table 15.

Although a step in the right direction, Mr. Cannon's report is in the form of general background information and apparently does not yet enter into the deliberations of the various committees. The "scorecard" suggested here might overcome that hurdle if it were in the form of an official communication presented to each congressional committee whenever it was about to consider a specific item of legislation containing financial authorization.

Choice of Budget Concept

Because the amount of money expended by the Federal Government during any given period is a matter of political controversy as well as economic analysis, several different methods of measuring the level of government spending have come into use. As will be demonstrated subsequently, the selection of a budget concept may in some circumstances significantly alter conclusions concerning the Federal Government's financial activities.

The three most widely used measures of federal spending are budget expenditures, cash payments to the public, and federal expenditures on income and product account (see Figure 4).

Budget expenditures. The most widely reported of the three series, budget expenditures, are computed on the basis of the administrative, or conventional, budget. This covers generally the government funds which are or can be subject to annual executive and legislative control.

The "budget expenditures" generally include all expenditures of the federal departments and agencies, plus the net outlays of the enterprises which are wholly owned by the Federal Government. They exclude the transactions of government-sponsored enterprises and trust funds and payments for retiring, purchasing, or redeeming the government's debt. This treatment is similar to that of many business firms whose budgets usually exclude the company pension funds and the operations of firms in which they only have a partial interest.

For the government enterprises which are included, usually only the net expenditures—the difference between gross disbursements and gross receipts—are reported in the total of budget expenditures. A number of exceptions, however, exist to this "net" treatment of government enterprises. Some government agencies which are not financially organized as business-type enterprises, notably the power marketing agencies of the Department of the Interior, deposit the proceeds from their operations directly into the Treasury. In such cases, these receipts do not offset budget expenditures but increase the totals of budget receipts. Either treatment has the same effect on the budget surplus or deficit.

Through the years, the items included in the budget totals have varied considerably. The more important changes are mentioned as an indication of the possibilities for future changes and improvements.

A number of items previously included on both the income and outgo sides have been gradually excluded. Beginning in 1948, capital transfers, such as payments to the Treasury by wholly owned government corporations for retirement of capital stock, have been excluded from both budget receipts and expenditures. Starting the following year, amounts refunded by the government, principally for overpayment of taxes, have been reported as deductions from total receipts rather than as budget expenditures.

Prior to 1953, the payroll taxes collected for the railroad retirement trust fund were included as budget receipts. The transfers of these receipts to the trust fund were also included as budget expenditures. They are now netted out of budget receipts and do not appear in budget expenditures. The exclusion of these items from both the receipt and expenditure totals has no effect on the budget surplus or deficit.

Cash payments to the public. The most comprehensive of the three measures of government spending, cash payments, are computed on the basis of what has come to be called the consolidated cash budget. Essentially, this measures the total flow of cash, exclusive of borrowing and the repayment of borrowing, between the government and the public. The public in this sense includes business firms, individuals, state and local governments, foreign governments, and international agencies. Cash payments include the operations of the many trust funds of the government, such as those for social security and unemployment compensation, and the operations of government-sponsored enterprises in which the Federal Government has had a share of ownership from time to time. The latter include the Banks for Cooperatives, Federal Home Loan Banks, and Federal Deposit Insurance Corporation.

Federal expenditures on income and product account. The newest of the three measures, federal expenditures on income and product account, represents the total of all the portions of federal spending that are included in the Gross National Product or related statistics. This measure includes direct purchases from business, transfer payments to individuals, and grants-in-aid to state and local governments. It excludes such capital items as loans and purchases of land and other existing assets.

The practical importance of the differences among these series may be illustrated with reference to the federal budget for the fiscal year 1964. The Budget Message states (pages 9-10):

> In presenting the budget as the Government's financial plan for 1964, I am giving major emphasis to a consolidated cash presentation, covering not only the administrative budget but also other Federal activities . . . . This provides a much more complete picture of governmental activities and finances than the administrative budget.

Nevertheless, later in the Message, the claim is made that the total of administrative budget expenditures for all programs (except national security, space, and interest) estimated for 1964 "has been held slightly below the 1963 level" (page 15). Technically, of course, the claim is correct. However, if, in keeping with the quotation above, the comparison were made on the basis of the cash budget, the claim would not have been supported. Cash payments (excepting national security, space, and interest) were estimated to rise from the fiscal year 1963 to 1964.

The illustration cited above is hardly unique. The availability of a variety of budget series lends itself to selective utilization to prove a given point or contention. It would appear more desir-

Figure 4

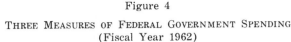

THREE MEASURES OF FEDERAL GOVERNMENT SPENDING
(Fiscal Year 1962)

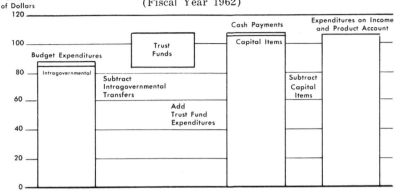

Note: Several adjustment items were too small to be charted: noncash budget expenditures (deducted to reach cash payments); government-sponsored enterprise expenditures (added to reach cash payments); miscellaneous adjustments for timing, netting and consolidation, and coverage (made in order to reach income and product expenditures).

able to have one standard measure of federal expenditures (and revenues), such as the cash budget, and to relegate other series to the subordinate status of subsidiary statements and special analyses.

This study is based on the concept of Federal Government cash payments to the public because, as demonstrated in Figure 4, it is the most comprehensive of the three available measures of government spending. Unlike the administrative budget, it includes the governmental trust funds which comprise the large and growing social security systems. Similarly, unlike the national income series, the cash payment concept includes important capital transactions such as the government lending programs.

SUMMARY AND CONCLUSIONS

PERSONS AND GROUPS concerned with budget policy—be their primary interest economy or efficiency in government operations or the use of fiscal policy to promote economic growth and stability—quickly encounter numerous legal and institutional obstacles to budgetary improvements. This study dealt with these obstacles and suggested several lines of potential improvement.

The Concentration of Pressures

Federal expenditures are very unevenly divided among the population, whether the category of analysis used is type of expenditure, location of the government activity, or the industries or groups that are benefited.

• Over 68 percent of the estimated Federal Government cash payments to the public in the fiscal year 1964 were devoted to national defense and health-labor-welfare programs.

• Over 90 percent of the contracts awarded by the Federal Government are currently being devoted to military and space programs.

• In the case of seven states—Kansas, California, Washington, New Mexico, Connecticut, Arizona, and Utah—work on defense contracts alone accounts for 20 to 30 percent of the total industrial employment.

• For individual industries, sales to the Federal Government range from 10 to 95 percent of the total.

For the individual locality, the variety of federal "largesse" which may be available, and competed for against other areas, is almost staggering. For example, 33 different federal "developmental" programs were conducted in the Atlanta metropolitan area in 1962, ranging from urban renewal and construction of roads and public buildings to saline water research and investigation of fish and wildlife.

The Mechanics of Government Spending

An examination of the entire sequence of the Federal Government spending process reveals certain key points of control, including some which are not normally regarded as part of the budget system proper.

• The enactment by the Congress of basic legislation authorizing a given government activity to be performed.

Although not a part of the formal budget process, this step comes closest to being the birth stage of government spending. In many cases, such legislation actually contains financial authorizations, bypassing the appropriations review.

• The screening of departmental budget requests by the Bureau of the Budget and the President.

- The review and approval of appropriation requests by the Congress.

The appropriation subcommittees of the Senate and House of Representatives perform the most detailed and important review. The key point of effective budgetary control by the Congress is the granting of new obligational authority, which empowers the government agencies to set in motion a chain of action that ultimately will result in a flow of expenditures.

- The apportionment of funds by the Bureau of the Budget.

The apportionment authority can be used to keep expenditures for a given activity below the level funded by the Congress.

- The payments by the Treasury.

Although this is the stage of the process on which public interest is normally focused for the control of government spending, it is the least effective of the various points of control. Generally, if a commitment has been made and costs incurred, the most that can be done at this stage is to postpone an expenditure.

Built-In Rigidities

An examination of the proposed budget for the fiscal year 1964 reveals that only 58 percent of the funds requested were subject to effective congressional review through the appropriations process. The remaining 42 percent consisted primarily of permanent indefinite appropriations, continuing construction projects, and other items relatively fixed or uncontrollable as a result of substantive legislation on the books.

- On the average, 96 percent of the budgets of the military and other national security programs for fiscal 1964 were subject to effective review. However, only 23 percent of the other agency budgets, the various domestic civilian programs, were actually subject to effective review.

- The bulk of the expenditures for the civilian, welfare agencies is authorized virtually automatically as a result of the basic, continuing commitments contained in statutes generally written by and reported out by committees of the Congress concerned with the individual program or group being benefited rather than with the state of federal finances.

• The various types of permanent budgetary commitments— such as fixed dollar amounts for certain grants to states or indefinite appropriation for given programs of the proceeds from whole categories of revenues—bear little if any relationship to the current requirements for federal expenditures. It was suggested that these commitments be reviewed in an attempt to eliminate them or at least convert them to permissive, authorizing legislation which would require annual congressional action on appropriation requests. There was a further suggestion of the desirability of an exhaustive re-examination of all basic laws creating fixed-cost obligations, with particular reference to terms and conditions under which the obligations accrue.

Proposed new expenditure programs provided for by the proposed 1964 budget were listed for the purpose of illustrating the great variety of these potential additions to the "uncontrollable area" of the budget.

The Choice Among Alternatives

It also was suggested that the budget recommendations be submitted and reviewed within a framework which would permit choices among alternatives—the conscious allocation of budget funds among the major purposes of government. Such a systematic approach is not now discernible within the budget process. An attempt to outline such an allocative framework for the 1964 budget revealed that:

• A large portion, but less than half, of the budgeted expenditures were devoted to the national security.

• The great bulk of all nondefense spending was allocated to the various welfare programs.

• About one-fifth of the funds for national security do not go directly to the U. S. Armed Forces, but are devoted to nonmilitary forms of competition or to foreign aid. (This was an example, among many, of a situation wherein the government conducts a variety of programs to achieve the same objective but does not compare directly the efficiency of the allocation of funds among these alternative means to a given end.)

The essential question to be considered is: "Would an extra dollar be more wisely spent for Program A or for Program B?" This fundamental question implicit in the allocation of budgeted funds is not raised in the overall budgetary process at present. Yet it is no more novel than a family's decision to use the Christmas bonus for a new car or a vacation, or a company's decision to use an increase in earnings to raise the dividend rate or to embark upon a new research program.

Improvements in Budget-Control Techniques

Because of renewed interest in the problems of federal expenditure control, plans that have been proposed in the past for improvements in budget reviewing techniques were reviewed. Finally, a procedure was suggested, as a step in the direction of such improvements, in the form of a "Budgetary Scorecard." The suggested scorecard is intended as a procedural means of enabling congressional committees and subcommittees, and the Congress as a whole, to focus attention on the total budget picture as actions are taken on individual bills appropriating funds or creating new expenditure programs.

APPENDIX A
GLOSSARY OF FEDERAL BUDGET TERMINOLOGY

Allotment—An authorization by the head or other authorized employee of a Federal Government agency to incur obligations within a specified amount pursuant to an appropriation or other statutory provision.

Apportionment—A distribution made by the Bureau of the Budget of amounts available for obligation or expenditure in an appropriation or fund account into amounts available for specified time periods, activities, functions, projects, or objects. The amounts so apportioned limit the obligations to be incurred or, when so specified, expenditures to be accrued.

Appropriation—A statutory authorization to make payments out of the Treasury for specified purposes.

Appropriation or fund account—An account established to make amounts available for obligation and expenditure from the Treasury. These accounts include not only those to which money is directly appropriated, but also revolving funds and trust funds.

A *one-year account* is one which is available for the incurring of obligations only during a specified fiscal year.

A *multiple-year account* is one which is available for the incurring of obligations for a definite period in excess of one fiscal year.

A *no-year account* is one which is available for the incurring of obligations for an indefinite period of time.

Authorization to expend from debt receipts—A statutory authorization to make payments for specified purposes out of moneys derived from the sales of securities rather than through direct appropriations (this differs from receipts from operations which are handled differently by the various agencies).

An *authorization to expend from public debt receipts* relates to moneys derived from the sale of public debt securities of the Federal Government.

An *authorization to expend from corporate debt receipts* relates to moneys derived from the sale of corporate debt securities.

Contract authorization—A statutory authorization under which contracts or other obligations may be entered into prior to an appropriation for the payment of such obligations.

Fiscal year—The period beginning July 1 and ending June 30 of the following calendar year. The fiscal year is designated by the calendar year in which it ends, e.g., the fiscal year 1964 is the year beginning July 1, 1963, and ending June 30, 1964.

Fund, trust—A fund established to account for the receipts which are held in trust for use in carrying out specific purposes and programs in accordance with an agreement or a statute.

New obligational authority—The sum of new authorizations to incur obligations. New obligational authority includes appropriations other than appropriations to liquidate contract authorizations, contract authorizations, authorizations to expend from debt receipts and authorizations which continue available any unobligated balances of these authorizations which were made for current operations of the year and which would otherwise expire for obligation purposes.

A *definite authorization* is one the amount of which is stated as a specific sum at the time the authorization is made (whether in an appropriation act or other law).

An *indefinite authorization* is one the amount of which is not stated as a specific sum when the authorization is made, but is determinable only at some future date, such as an appropriation of all or part of the receipts from a certain source.

A *permanent authorization* is one automatically made each year over a period of time by virtue of standing legislation, without annual action by Congress.

A *current authorization* is one enacted by Congress in or immediately preceding the fiscal year.

Obligations incurred—Amounts of orders placed, contracts awarded, services received, and similar transactions during a given period requiring disbursement of money. They include disbursements not preceded by the recording of obligations.

Reserves, budgetary—Portions of appropriations, funds, or contract authorizations set aside by the Bureau of the Budget for (a) savings which are made possible by or through changes in requirements, greater efficiency of operations, or other developments subsequent to the date on which the authorization was made available, and (b) contingencies.

APPENDIX B
DETAILED PROGRAM COMPOSITION OF THE
1964 BUDGET[1]

NEW OBLIGATIONAL AUTHORITY
(millions of dollars)

NATIONAL SECURITY

	Amount	Comment
U. S. Military Forces		
Department of Defense	$49,989	Covers all of the traditional military functions of the DOD except retired pay and family housing
Atomic Energy Commission....	1,446	Assumed at one-half of total AEC budget
Selective Service System	38	Military personnel acquisition
Subtotal	$51,473	

[1] In the form as first submitted in January 1963.

	Amount	Comment
U. S. Passive Defense		
Office of Emergency Planning	18	Civil defense
Department of Defense	300	Civil defense activities
Subtotal	$ 318	
Foreign Military Forces		
Military assistance	$ 1,480	Military portion of foreign aid program
Foreign Non-Military Activities		
Foreign assistance—economic	$ 4,421	All
Peace Corps	108	All
International Financial Insti-		
tutions	112	U. S. contribution to Inter-American Development Bank, etc.
Department of Defense	48	Panama Canal, etc.
Subtotal	$ 4,689	
Arms Control and Disarmament		
U. S. Arms Control and Dis-		
armament Agency	$ 15	All
Political and Psychological		
Competition		
U. S. Information Agency......	$ 217	All
Scientific Competition		
National Aeronautics and		
Space Administration	$ 5,712	All
Total, National Security..	$63,904	

PUBLIC WELFARE

	Amount	Comment
Life Insurance and Retirement		
Programs		
Department of Defense	$ 1,163	Retired pay
Department of Health, Educa-		
tion, and Welfare	16,822	Old-age, survivors and disability insurance system
Veterans Administration	758	National Service Life Insurance
Railroad Retirement Board....	1,231	Railroad Retirement System
The Judiciary	1	} Government employees retirement systems
Department of State	8	
Civil Service Commsson	2,331	
Subtotal	$22,314	

	Amount	Comment
Unemployment Insurance		
Department of Labor	$ 4,407	Unemployment trust fund
Health		
Department of Health, Education, and Welfare	$ 1,861	Public Health Service, etc.
Treasury Department	5	Narcotics Bureau
Veterans Administration	1,218	Veterans' medical program
Subtotal	$ 3,084	
Public Assistance		
Department of Health, Education and Welfare	$ 3,119	Grants to states for public assistance
Veterans Administration	1,800	Pensions for veterans without service-connected disabilities
Subtotal	$ 4,919	
Veterans Compensation		
Veterans Administration	$ 2,061	Compensation for service-connected disabilities
Assistance to Farmers and Rural Areas		
Department of Agriculture....	$ 7,227	Farm price supports and other subsidies
Department of the Interior......	63	Shared revenues with local governments
Subtotal	$ 7,290	
Urban Housing and Facilities		
Department of Defense	$ 734	Family housing
Housing and Home Financing Agency	932	All, except urban transportation
National Capital Planning Commission	1	All
Subtotal	$ 1,667	
Miscellaneous Welfare		
Disaster Relief	$ 20	All
Transitional Grants to Alaska	3	All
Department of Defense	18	Cemeterial expenses
Department of Health, Education, and Welfare	21	Juvenile delinquency, etc.
Department of the Interior......	216	Indian welfare
Department of Labor	356	Manpower training, etc.
Treasury Department	34	Aid to Puerto Rico
Veterans Administration	473	Administrative expenses
American Battle Monuments Commission	2	All
Subtotal	$ 1,143	
Total, Public Welfare..	46,885	

Economic Development

	Amount	Comment
Natural Resources		
Department of Agriculture....	$ 879	Forest Service and Soil Conservation
Department of Defense	1,104	Corps of Engineers
Department of the Interior......	1,010	Water, power, recreation, etc.
Atomic Energy Commission....	1,447	One-half of total
TVA	44	All
Subtotal	$ 4,484	
Transportation Facilities		
Department of Commerce	$ 3,772	Mainly highways
Department of the Interior......	18	Indian roads
Treasury Department	364	Coast Guard
Federal Aviation Agency........	810	All
Housing and Home Finance Agency	100	Urban transportation
National Capital Transportation Agency	2	All
Subtotal	$ 5,066	
Education and General Research		
Department of Commerce........	$ 148	Standards, Geological Survey, etc.
Department of Health, Education, and Welfare	2,082	Office of Education, etc.
Department of Labor	20	Economic research
National Science Foundation..	589	All
Subtotal	$ 2,839	
Economic Regulation		
Department of Agriculture......	$ 1	Commodity Exchange Authority
Department of the Interior....	1	Oil and gas regulation
Department of Justice	7	Antitrust
Department of Labor	30	Wages, hours, reports, etc.
CAB	11	All (except subsidies)
FCC	17	All
Federal Maritime Commission	3	All
FPC	13	All
FTC	13	All
ICC	25	All
NLRB	23	All
Renegotiation Board	3	All
SEC	14	All
Tariff Commission	3	All
Subtotal	$ 164	
Aids and Subsidies to Businesses		
Department of Agriculture...,.	$ 87	Statistics, etc.
Department of Commerce........	776	Maritime, etc.

	Amount	Comment
Department of the Interior......	5	Lead and zinc subsidies
Department of Labor	1	Mexican farm labor
Post Office Department............	565	Postal deficit
CAB	83	Airline subsidy
Farm Credit Administration...	3	All
Federal Mediation and Conciliation Service	6	All
National Mediation Board......	2	
Small Business Administration	215	All
Subtotal	$ 1,743	
Total, Economic Development	$14,296	

GOVERNMENT OPERATIONS

Interest Payments		
Treasury Department	$10,103	Mainly interest on the public debt
Legislative Functions		
Legislative Branch	$ 123	All (except Government Printing Office)
Judicial and Law Enforcement		
The Judiciary	$ 69	All
Department of Justice	348	All (except anti-trust)
Treasury Department	10	Secret Service
Commission on Civil Rights....	1	All
Tax Court	2	All
Subtotal	$ 430	
Housekeeping Functions		
Executive Office of the President	$ 15	All (except OEP)
President's Emergency Fund..	1	All
Legislative Branch	27	Government Printing Office
Treasury Department	802	Tax collection, check payments, etc.
General Services Administration	659	All
Civil Service Commission	49	All
Foreign Claims Settlement Commission	50	All
GAO	47	All
Smithsonian Institution	24	All
Miscellaneous Agencies	2	All
District of Columbia	452	All
Undistributed Pay Increases..	200	All
Contingencies	250	All
Subtotal	$ 2,578	

	Amount	Comment
Conducting Foreign Relations		
Department of the Interior....	$ 36	Trust territories, etc.
Department of Labor	1	Foreign labor exchanges
Department of State	374	All
Subtotal	$ 411	
Total, Government Operations	13,645	
GRAND TOTAL......	$138,730	

Source: *The Budget of the United States Government for the Fiscal year Ending June 30, 1964* (Washington: U. S. Government Printing Office, 1963), pp. 128-321.

BIBLIOGRAPHY

Edward C. Banfield. "Congress and the Budget: A Planner's Criticism," *American Political Science Review*, December 1949.

Gerhard Colm with the assistance of Marilyn Young. *The Federal Budget and the National Economy*, National Planning Association, Planning Pamphlet No. 90, March 1955.

Otto Eckstein. "Evaluation of Federal Expenditures for Water Resource Projects," in U. S. Congress, Joint Economic Committee, *Federal Expenditure Policy for Economic Growth and Stability* (Washington: U. S. Government Printing Office, 1957.)

Joseph P. Harris. "Needed Reforms in the Federal Budget System," *Public Administration Review*, Autumn 1952.

I. M. Labovitz. *Federal Revenues and Expenditures in the Several States, Averages for the Fiscal Years 1959-61* (Washington: Library of Congress, September 19, 1962).

Eva Mueller. "Public Attitudes Toward Fiscal Programs," *Quarterly Journal of Economics*, May 1963.

David Novick. "Planning Ahead in the Department of Defense," *California Management Review*, Summer 1963.

Arthur Smithies. *The Budgetary Process in the United States* (New York: McGraw-Hill Book Co., 1955).

U. S. Commission on Organization of the Executive Branch of the Government. *Budgeting and Accounting* (Washington: U. S. Government Printing Office, 1949).

U. S. President. *The Budget of the United States Government for the Fiscal Year Ending June 30, 1964* (Washington: U. S. Government Printing Office, 1963 [including Appendix]).

U. S. Senate, Committee on Government Operations. *Role of the Federal Government in Metropolitan Areas* (Washington: U. S. Government Printing Office, 1963).

Robert A. Wallace. *Congressional Control of Federal Spending* (Detroit: Wayne State University Press, 1960).

Murray L. Weidenbaum. "The Economic Impact of the Government Spending Process," *The Business Review*, The University of Houston, Spring 1961.

THE RESPONSIBLE USE OF POWER

A CRITICAL ANALYSIS OF THE CONGRESSIONAL BUDGET PROCESS

By

JOHN S. SALOMA III

INTRODUCTION

In the closing minutes of the first session of the Eighty-eighth Congress, Clarence Cannon, the venerable 84-year old chairman of the House Committee on Appropriations, chided his colleagues for "hacking at the branches" of federal spending instead of attacking the roots. In terse and pointed language he reminded the House that "the machinery is at hand. It needs no reform. All we need is the will, the disposition to do it. . . . The only way to restrain spending is to stop authorizing more, stop asking for more, stop appropriating more. There is no other way." [1]

The view of the late chairman of House Appropriations, i.e., that there is nothing basically wrong with

[1] *Congressional Record,* 88th Congress, 1st Session, December 30, 1963, p. 24378.

congressional procedures for considering the executive budget but that Congress suffers from a lack of self-discipline, is shared by many members of the appropriations committees and the Congress at large. Yet a review of the congressional record in controlling expenditures and the several unsuccessful efforts to reform congressional fiscal machinery suggests that the problem is far more deeply rooted. George Galloway, the dean of congressional scholars, has concluded that of the many reforms attempted in the Legislative Reorganization Act of 1946, those dealing with fiscal control have been the most disappointing.[2]

This study is a critical analysis of the congressional budget process. Its primary focus is the authorization-appropriations phase of the overall federal budget process, although it is also concerned with revenue actions, the congressional review function in the expenditure of funds, and with the broader economic implications of congressional budgetary decisions. The analysis is both descriptive and prescriptive. It starts with an empirical definition of the congressional budget system, the historical determinants in its development, and contemporary roles of the principal actors in the process.

Then a number of common and recurring criticisms of the system are examined and evaluated in a further description of the congressional budget process as it actually functions. Next, the major attempts to reform the system are analyzed and the reasons for their relative success or failure assessed. From these initial sections of the study a strategy for fiscal reform is developed.

This study, while serving in the broader sense as a case study in the development of relations between the legislative and executive branches, is primarily concerned with the uses of congressional power. It asks the question "How can congressional power be used more responsibly and constructively in the determination of national policy?"

The study concludes that Congress should seek four goals in its consideration of the budget: (1) economy and efficiency in governmental operations; (2) surveillance or "oversight" of the bureaucracy; (3) review of overall fiscal policy, and (4) intelligent budgetary control based on adequate information.

To accomplish these objectives:

—Congress should establish a Joint Committee on Fiscal Policy

---

[2] "Operation of Legislative Reorganization Act of 1946," reprinted in Senate, Committee on Expenditures in the Executive Departments, *Hearings, Organization and Operation of Congress: Evaluation of the Effects of Laws Enacted to Reorganize the Legislative Branch of the Government,* 82d Congress, 1st Session, 1951, p. 641.

—Congress should exert more control at the authorization stage of the budgetary process

—The appropriations committees should provide for a more integrated review of the budget

—The appropriations committees should increase their staffs to develop adequate information for appropriation decisions

—The appropriations committees should make more effective use of the expenditure analysis and review accomplished by the committees on government operations and the General Accounting Office

—Congress should provide means for more intelligent partisan debate on the budget

—Congress should develop a Budget Information Service, and

—Congress should improve the scheduling of the congressional budget process.

I.

THE CONGRESSIONAL BUDGET PROCESS

The American budgetary process should be viewed as a working example of the separation of powers. While we have grown accustomed to calling the budget the executive budget or the President's budget due to the initiating role of the executive, Congress occupies a strategic constitutional position in the total budgetary system. Article I, section 8 of the Constitution gives Congress the specific power to lay and collect taxes, to borrow money on the credit of the United States and to coin money. Article I, section 9, clause 7 requires that "no money shall be drawn from the treasury but in consequence of appropriation made by law." The American Constitution by at once separating and blending the processes of legislation, administration, and adjudication has introduced an element of indeterminateness to the functioning of our government.[1] As we might expect the executive and legislative roles in the budgetary process have not been static or for that matter clearly delineated over time. The objective of this introductory section is to define the contemporary roles of the major actors in the budgetary system (with some attention to historical deveopment)[2] and to describe the major characteristics of the congressional components of the budgetary process.[3]

Legislative and Executive Roles in the Budget Process

The budget process may be resolved into three major phases: formulation of the executive budget, congressional action on appropriations, and execution of the enacted budget (see Figure I). A complete cycle of the budget process for one fiscal year extends over approximately 30 months, with initial planning begun 16 months before the start of the fiscal year. Since passage of the Budget and Account-

---

[1] David B. Truman concludes that under the "magnificent ambiguities" of the Constitution it is never clear whether the President or a transient majority in the Congress is to exercise control over the units of the executive branch. "The separation of powers and the system of checks and balances leave open a series of alternative approaches to the government; a number of key points of decision are established in parallel with no formal, solid basis of hierarchy among them." *The Governmental Process: Political Interests and Public Opinion* (New York: Alfred A. Knopf, 1951), p. 401.

[2] For a concise history of major relevant legislation see Senate, Committee on Government Operations, *Financial Management in the Federal Government*, 87th Congress, 1st Session, 1961, Senate Document 11, esp. pp. 3-108. More interpretative accounts are given by Lucius Wilmerding, Jr., *The Spending Power: A History of the Efforts of Congress to Control Expenditures* (New Haven: Yale University Press, 1943), and Arthur Smithies, *The Budgetary Process in the United States* (New York: McGraw-Hill, 1955; Committee for Economic Development Research Study), esp. pp. 49-100. For a description of the various committees in the system, especially the revenue and credit committees, see Ralph K. Huitt, "Congressional Organization and Operations in the Field of Money and Credit," in William Fellner, *et al., Fiscal and Debt Management Policies: A Series of Research Studies prepared for the Commission on Money and Credit* (Englewood Cliffs, N.J.: Prentice-Hall, 1963), pp. 399-495.

[3] Richard Fenno's work on the House Appropriations Committee is the first serious study of the key element in the system. Part of his forthcoming study has appeared as a journal article. See "The House Appropriations Committee as a Political System: The Problem of Integration," *American Political Science Review*, June 1962, pp. 310-24. A refreshing approach to budgetary theory is found in some recent research by Aaron Wildavsky. See *The Politics of the Budgetary Process* (Boston: Little, Brown and Company, 1964). For a case study of the budgetary process, see Warner R. Schilling, "The Politics of National Defense: Fiscal 1950," in Warner R. Schilling, Paul Y. Hammond, and Glenn H. Snyder, *Strategy, Politics, and Defense Budgets* (New York: Columbia University Press, 1962).

ing Act of 1921, the Bureau of the Budget has been charged with the responsibility of formulating an executive budget for the President. The executive has insisted on "the integrity of the executive budget" during formulation and has developed an exclusive role in this presubmission phase, i.e., limiting participation effectively to the President, Bureau of the Budget, and the executive agencies. In the appropriations or budget review phase, the process of budget formulation is re-enacted on a smaller scale, with congressional actors in the dominant roles. In the execution phase the Bureau of the Budget and executive agencies resume major active roles while Congress, with the assistance of the General Accounting Office, reviews the process of expenditure. It required well over 100 years, from the breakdown of Hamilton's initial efforts in the 1790's until the creation of a Bureau of the Budget within the executive, before. this balance of roles was achieved. In fact, one can speak of a "budget process" in only the loosest sense during the nineteenth century.

The basic ground rules for the executive and legislature in fiscal affairs were defined with the defeat of the Federalists by the Jeffersonians at the turn of the century. Hamiltonian finance had emphasized *executive discretion,* with general appropriations being in lump sums, and with broad construction by the Secretary of the Treasury of any legislative restrictions. At the same time Hamilton attempted to establish a close working relationship with the Congress in the capacity of a Minister of Finance. With Federalist control of both branches he met with initial success. A House Committee on Ways and Means, established in July 1789, was "discharged" in September of that year from further consideration of financial matters which were then referred to the Secretary of the Treasury. A series of directives issued to Hamilton by the first Congress suggest how fully he succeeded in instituting himself as "agent and adviser" to Congress in matters pertaining to public finance and the national economy.[4] Hamilton was not slow to perceive the ambiguities of and opportunities afforded by the separation of powers, and he developed his dual role as Secretary of the Treasury with some skill.[5]

In opposition to Hamilton, the Jeffersonians led by Albert Gallatin in the House defined a theory of

[4] See George Galloway, *History of the House of Representatives* (New York: Thomas Y. Crowell, 1962), pp. 17-18.

[5] See Wilfred E. Binkley, *President and Congress* (New York: Alfred A. Knopf, 1947), chap. ii, "The Solution of the Federalist Party," pp. 26-48.

legislative restraint, or limitation of executive discretion, through the imposition of specific appropriations. The motivation for the Jeffersonian attack had several aspects. Hamilton's financial reforms had mobilized political opposition in the country and the Jeffersonians' first position of strength was in the popularly elected House.[6] An attack on Hamilton accorded both with party principle and political expediency. Specific appropriations could be used to embarrass the President and his party, a point the Federalists were just as willing to exploit when Jefferson occupied the presidency![7]

But more basic was the development of an independent congressional role. Hamilton's experiment with a form of cabinet government could not last for long; it did not survive the first change in party control. Congress moved slowly toward the creation of a system of standing committees. A House Committee on Ways and Means was appointed in December 1795 under a resolution introduced by Gallatin. Gallatin then proceeded from his position on the committee—which considered both revenue and appropriations measures—to offer a series of amendments for specific appropria-

tions to be "solely applied to the objects for which they are respectively appropriated."[8] However, the Senate was generally reluctant to forbid the "mingling of appropriations" or transfer of funds between appropriation items by the executive and by the time Jefferson came to office in 1801 the practice of transfer—in spite of legislative prohibitions—was firmly established.

Under Jefferson the basic doctrines of "legislative restraint" were articulated. At the suggestion of Gallatin, now his Secretary of the Treasury, Jefferson included the following passage in his first communication to Congress:

> In our care, too, of the public contributions intrusted to our direction it would be prudent to multiply barriers against their dissipation by appropriating specific sums to every specific purpose susceptible of definition; by disallowing all applications of money varying from the appropriation in object or transcending it in amount; by reducing the undefined field of contingencies and thereby circumscribing discretionary powers over money. . . .[9]

[6] Wilfred E. Binkley, *American Political Parties: Their Natural History* (New York: Alfred A. Knopf, 1943), pp. 62-71.
[7] Wilmerding, *op. cit.,* pp. 61-63.
[8] *Ibid.,* chap. ii, "Gallatin and the Struggle with Wolcott: 1789-1801."
[9] Cited in Wilmerding, *op. cit.,* pp. 50-51.

Jefferson, however, ignored an earlier proviso that Gallatin had made. Since it would be impossible to foresee, in all its details, the necessary application of funds, the Secretary of the Treasury had warned, Congress should grant the executive departments "a reasonable discretion" by avoiding too detailed appropriations. Other Jeffersonians in subsequent years were also to disregard this warning as they proceeded to erect barrier after barrier against the discretionary powers of the executive.

Several conclusions emerge from the post-Jeffersonian experience in fiscal control. First, after the repudiation of the Hamiltonian experiment, Congress assumed the dominant role. It was commonly accepted that Congress had the exclusive power of appropriation—and that this power included the right to specify the objects of appropriation and the amounts to be applied to each object. The exercise of this power was frequent, although it was not carried to its logical extreme until the post-Civil War period—the zenith of congressional ascendancy.

Second, according to the accepted doctrine of legislative restraint, the executive was obliged to follow the spending directives of Congress, and to depart from specified appropriations only under circumstances of national emergency. Congress would make subsequent adjustments in such an event. In theory, budget formulation was the province of the legislature, execution *without* discretion the assignment of the executive.

Third, in practice the executive proceeded to develop a variety of techniques or devices to achieve *de facto* if illegal discretionary powers. The practice of transferring appropriations was inherited from the Federalist period. As Congress attempted to close loopholes one by one, the executive agencies would discover or invent new ones: carrying forward unexpended balances of old appropriations, contracting in anticipation of contracts, and ultimately instituting the coercive deficiency. At times of emergency, war, and economic crisis Congress agreed to a further loosening of its control by authorizing lump sum appropriations, transfers, the use of revolving funds, direct Treasury borrowing, and the establishment of independent governmental authorities or corporations.

Fourth, periodic congressional attempts to enforce specific appropriations rigorously ended in failure, resulting in loss of congressional control of the budget process. The decade from 1868-78 serves as a case in point. Legislation in 1868, 1870, and 1874 systematically prohibited all the major discretionary devices used by the executive agencies before and during the Civil War. This congressional rigor when combined with the practice of underappropriation forced the agencies to resort to coercive deficiencies. Deficiency appropriations were not new, having been used recurringly by the Navy in Jefferson's Administration. John Randolph, chairman of Ways and Means, warned the House in 1806 that appropriations had become "a matter of form, or less than a shadow of a shade, a mere cobweb against expenditures." Congress specified limits; but what good did it do if the agency behaved like "a saucy boy who knows that his grandfather will gratify him, and over-runs the sum allowed him at pleasure."[10] Now, as deficiencies became habitual, Randolph's worst fears were realized. Annual appropriations were accepted by the agencies as only partial. Since Congress could not afford to terminate essential services (the agencies were not hesitant to use forms of blackmail), supplemental appropriations would be granted.[11] Agencies based their expenditures not on the initial

sums appropriated by Congress but on what they thought the congressional market would bear. With the continuing disintegration of the congressional budget process, the agencies became the effective appropriating authorities, congressional control a mere cobweb. The problem of deficiencies, even with the adoption of anti-deficiency legislation in 1906, continued to plague the Congress and was one of the factors contributing to congressional support for the major budgetary reforms in 1921.

Fifth, against this background of conflict of legislative and executive roles, the congressional machinery for budgetary control underwent a steady process of disintegration over the course of the century. The initial focus for congressional participation in the budget process had been the House Committee on Ways and Means, with its powers over revenue and appropriations bills. In January 1802 the powers of the Committee were increased to permit examination of the application by the departments of appropriated funds (i.e., a post-audit function to complement congres-

---

[10] *Ibid.*, pp. 66-67. See also chap. vii, "The Fight Against Deficiencies: 1879-1917."

[11] There were other reasons for congressional impotence. The disintegration of the congressional budget process (described below) coincided with this period. L. D. White observes that "there was a ready acquiescence on the part of individual Congressmen or party factions that wanted some particular payment made or task undertaken. The interests of the Congressmen were often different from and contrary to the interests of Congress." *The Jacksonians*, p. 141, cited by Galloway, *op. cit.* p. 176.

sional consideration and action on departmental estimates). However, the potential of what might have become the most powerful fiscal committee in the history of Congress did not materialize. Ways and Means soon discovered, as had earlier investigating committees, that the task of expenditure review and audit was too massive an undertaking for a committee of congressmen "having everything to learn, with the fragments of their hours" to accomplish.[12] Congress reacted to this failure by transferring, in 1814, the function of expenditure review to a new standing Committee on Public Expenditures. John Taylor indignantly observed that "the rat-catchers of former sessions" had not caught the animals, and that now it was Congress' turn to "not only ferret out the rats but hunt the lazy cats who let them live."[13] In 1816 the Committee on Public Expenditures was supplemented by six additional standing committees on expenditures (State,

Treasury, War, Navy, Post Office, and Public Buildings) as part of Henry Clay's plans for the assertion of congressional leadership. None of these committees or their successors was able to perform an audit function for Congress. This problem remained unresolved until the establishment of the General Accounting Office in the budgetary reforms of 1921.

During the first decades of the nineteenth century, the rationale for budgetary control — the need to weigh expenditures in light of anticipated revenues — was progressively undermined by a growing yield from the customs tariff and a chronic tendency toward a budget surplus.[14] This overall financial situation facilitated the congressional decision to divide the increasingly burdensome revenue and spending functions between Ways and Means and a new House Committee on Appropriations in 1865.[15] The Appropriations Committee under the strong leadership of Garfield and

[12] See remarks of Bayard, Federalist member of the Nicholson Committee, May 1802, cited in Wilmerding, *op. cit.,* pp. 204-06.

[13] *Ibid.,* pp. 207-08.

[14] See Smithies, *op. cit.,* pp. 58-62. Smithies notes that "one of the main conditions for over-all budgetary control was thus absent. . . . After all, budgeting is a problem of scarce resources and without scarcity budgeting has no functions. The nineteenth century experience thus left the Government ill-equipped to deal with twentieth-century budgetary issues."

[15] Ways and Means was also deprived of its credit functions at this time, which were vested in a new Banking and Currency Committee. Smithies observes that "the chronic surplus condition of the budget made it unnecessary for government borrowing to become a regular part of Federal finance." *Ibid,* p. 61.

Randall soon became dominant in the House. A rules change in 1876 permitted general legislation in appropriations bills insofar as it reduced expenditures.[16] This had the effect of overloading the appropriating process and extending the jurisdiction of the committee over the entire legislative field. In 1880, the Appropriations Committee was stripped of its jurisdiction over the Agriculture appropriation bill; in 1885, of its jurisdiction over the appropriation bills for Army, Navy, Indian Affairs, Foreign Affairs, and Rivers and Harbors. This reaction to the enormous power of Appropriations under Randall was to be expected but the dispersal of the appropriations power, when combined with the practice of excessive utilization of deficiency appropriating (which were ironically still under the control of the Appropriations Committee) led to virtually a complete breakdown of congressional control.[17] Nine committees of the House shared the authority to report appropriations bills until July 1920 when the House rules were amended to form a single Appropriations Committee.

This digression into the historical experience of the nineteenth century helps to explain the context within which the Budget and Accounting Act of 1921 was formulated and the legislative and executive roles in the budget process redefined. Congress, theoretically supreme, had permitted the executive agencies to determine appropriations in practice. The continued sense of frustration involved in efforts both to control estimates and to give adequate review to expenditures, together with a new budgetary situation at the end of the First World War, of which the keynote was "retrenchment," caused Congress to turn to new solutions. The return of the Republicans to office provided the final impetus in 1921 for putting government finances on a sound "business" basis. The approach taken was threefold: (1) fixing executive re-

---

[16] This rule, known as the "Holman Rule" or retrenchment rule was employed from 1876 to 1885 and amended to its present form in the 52d Congress. It was dropped during the 54th to 61st Congresses (1895-1911) but has been readopted by all subsequent Congresses.

[17] Wilmerding describes the resulting chaos as follows: ". . . the grasp which the Committee on Appropriations alone could keep upon the purse strings was relaxed; the spending committees, having intimate and for the most part cordial relations each with a particular department, launched out into an unrestrained competition for appropriations. . . . In these circumstances it is not surprising that executive dereliction passed almost unnoticed and that the department heads and bureau chiefs came to look upon themselves rather than upon Congress as the ultimate arbiters of expenditure. . . ." *Op. cit.,* pp. 143-44.

sponsibility for the estimates submitted to Congress (i.e., budget formulation), (2) creating a new governmental instrument for the audit of executive accounts, primarily responsible to the Congress, and (3) internal consolidation of the congressional budget system.

Representative James W. Good of Iowa, chairman of the House Select Committee established in 1919 to study the question of a federal budget system, explained the rationale for creating an executive budget and a special budget staff in the following terms:

> . . . the estimates of expenditure needs now submitted to Congress represent only the desires of the individual departments, establishments, and bureaus; . . . these requests have been subjected to no superior revision with a view to bringing them into harmony with each other, to eliminating duplication of organization or activities, or of making them, as a whole conform to the needs of the Nation as represented by the condition of the Treasury and respective revenues. . . .[18]

While Congress was not ceding its dominant position, it was enlisting the President's assistance in keeping the executive agencies under control. Good remarked that a great deal of time of the committees of Congress was consumed in "exploding the visionary schemes of bureau chiefs for which no administration would be willing to stand responsible."

Under the final provisions of the Budget and Accounting Act of 1921, the President was vested with the responsibility for transmitting a national budget to the Congress at the beginning of each session. He was also authorized to submit, at his discretion, supplemental or deficiency estimates made necessary by laws enacted after transmission of the budget or otherwise determined to be in the public interest.

A Bureau of the Budget, charged with the responsibility of preparing the budget for the President, was placed in the Department of the Treasury but headed by a Director of the Budget appointed by the President and directly responsible to him.

The Bureau as the President's agent was given authority under section 207 of the Act to "assemble, correlate, revise, reduce or increase" the estimates of the several departments and establishments. The Bureau also was empowered under section 209 to make detailed studies of the departments and establishments to enable the President to de-

---

[18] See *Congressional Record*, 66th Congress, 1st Session, October 17, 1919, pp. 7083ff.

termine what changes should be made in (1) existing organization and activities, (2) appropriations, (3) assignment of particular activities, and (4) regrouping of services.[19]

Congress also envisioned a broad role for the new General Accounting Office (GAO) in the budget process. While the primary intent was to equip Congress with an agent that could execute an independent audit of executive accounts—a function Congress had failed to perform in spite of numerous committees on expenditures it had established and charged with the task—it is also clear that Congress hoped to create a powerful new actor in the budgetary process. Representative Good told the House that he could conceive of "no official of the United States who [would] have more power than the comptroller general of the United States."[20] Under the Act as finally passed the GAO absorbed the powers and duties previously exercised by the Comptroller

of the Treasury and the six auditors of the Department of the Treasury. This included the power to settle or adjust all claims and demands, and the power to "investigate at the seat of government or elsewhere, all matters relating to the receipt, disbursement, and application of public funds" and to make regular reports to Congress with "recommendations looking to greater economy or efficiency in public expenditures."[21] But the Comptroller General was to be "something more than a bookkeeper or accountant." Good's contention that he should be a "real critic" with an independent voice and access to Congress at all times was amplified during the congressional debates.[22]

Congress obviously hoped that the GAO would solve the past dilemmas of fiscal control and that it would be more than a counterweight to the new Bureau of the Budget. Good anticipated three positive results.[23] First, the GAO would inform Congress as to "the actual con-

---

[19] The Bureau of the Budget was transferred to the Executive Office of the President by Executive Order 8248, September 8, 1939. For a discussion of the development of the Bureau since 1921, see Fritz Morstein Marx, "The Bureau of the Budget: Its Evolution and Present Role," *American Political Science Review,* August, October 1945, pp. 653-84, 869-98.

[20] *Congressional Record,* 66th Congress, 1st Session, October 18, 1919, p. 7132.

[21] Budget and Accounting Act of 1921, section 312.

[22] *Congressional Record,* 66th Congress, 1st Session, October 17, 1919, pp. 7084-86 and October 18, 1919, pp. 7131-32. For a summary of the debates see *Financial Management in the Federal Government,* Appendix B. Staff Memorandum No. 83-2-33 (historical data relating to the creation and functions of the Office of the Comptroller General).

[23] *Congressional Record,* 66th Congress, 1st Session, October 17, 1919, pp. 7085-86.

ditions" surrounding the expenditure of public funds in every department of the government. It would perform an intelligence function to discover the "very facts that Congress ought to be in possession of" in performing its constitutional duties. Second, it would serve as "a check on the President and those under him in the preparation of the budget." The implication was clear that representatives of the GAO would sit in appropriations hearings and assist the Congress in review of the budget.[24] Third, it would help Congress to locate waste and extravagant use of funds and to place responsibility on the appropriate cabinet officer. Representative Temple's observation that "the whole plan gets back to the scheme of the Constitution of the United States" and "restores something of the power that Congress formerly had . . . . but which in practice has been largely taken over by the executive"[25] was typical. The reforms of 1921 were not an abdication of powers to the executive but an effort to overcome the deficiencies of the past that had left Congress impotent. In the process both legislative and executive roles were to be strengthened. An assessment of the net effects of the reforms must await consideration of the third aspect of the reforms — internal consolidation of the congressional budget system.

During the considerations of the Select Committee in 1919 it was evident to all that Congress would have to put its own house in order if a new budget system were to function effectively. Representative Medill McCormick's plan for a national budget system was the most radical proposal seriously advanced. Under McCormick's proposals the House would reinstitute a single fiscal committee modeled on the old Ways and Means Committee. Estimates submitted by the executive could be raised only by a two-thirds vote of the committee; amendments to this effect would be ruled out of

[24] See Representative Good's remarks, *Congressional Record,* 66th Congress, 1st Session, May 3, 1921, p. 982. ". . . and when the committee from the bureau of the budget or the President's staff come and explain the budget, sitting right there, they are brought to face the comptroller general of the United States; and if a representative of the bureau of the budget states something that is not true, if he fails to state the whole truth the comptroller general sits there with the Committee on Appropriations as an arm of Congress and can supply the desired information." Some members were willing to give the GAO wide discretion in a pre-audit of appropriations. See Representative Taylor's comments, *Congressional Record,* 66th Congress, 1st Session, October 18, 1919, p. 7128. "They are responsible only to Congress. . . . They will have to be coldblooded and cut down appropriations in every direction that they deem proper. . . ." For a further discussion of the congressional mood see Wilmerding, *op. cit.,* pp. 267-71.

[25] *Congressional Record,* 66th Congress, 1st Session, October 20, 1919, p. 7211.

order on the floor of the House. Congress, as we have seen, took the more moderate approach of consolidating appropriation power under a single House Committee on Appropriations. Further rationalization of the congressional system came later. In December 1927, the House consolidated 11 separate committees on expenditures in the executive department — Clay's six and their progeny—into a single committee to examine the accounts and expenditures of the several departments of the government. (The Senate consolidated its committees two years later.) The new committee also provided a focus for the receipt of GAO audits and reports of investigation. In 1952 the committee was renamed the Committee on Government Operations.

Three other additions to the congressional machinery for considering the budget deserve mention at this point. The revenue committees were strengthened in 1926 with the creation of a Joint Committee on Internal Revenue Taxation, composed of five members each from the House Ways and Means and Senate Finance Committees. The Joint Committee has served as a mechanism for providing professional staff assistance to the two committees as well as a focus for congressional review of Treasury revenue estimates and revenue proposals in the executive budget.

The Joint Economic Committee, established as the Joint Committee on the Economic Report under the Employment Act of 1946, has provided the Congress with a broader perspective on national economic policy and the economic implications of the budget—but the committee is only loosely related to the formal congressional budget process.

Lastly, the Joint Committee on the Reduction of Non-essential Expenditures, established under the leadership of Senator Harry F. Byrd in 1941, completes the list of congressional participants in the budget process. It supplements (or "duplicates" if one prefers) the work of the Committees on Government Operations but includes in its membership the Secretary of the Treasury and the Budget Director. The Byrd Committee bears the distinct imprint of its creator and is likely to be absorbed into the existing congressional committee structure when the Senator retires from the congressional scene.

Further efforts at consolidation—notably the Joint Committee on the Legislative Budget and the Omnibus Appropriation Bill—have failed for reasons that will be analyzed presently.

*　　*　　*　　*　　*

In the period since 1921 the basic

allocation of roles between the executive and legislative branches has remained stable although differential development along the three avenues of reform — e x e c u t i v e budget formulation (the Bureau of the Budget), the development of the GAO as a congressional resource in the budgetary process, and internal congressional reform of the fiscal committees—has produced an emphasis not anticipated by the reformers of the period. The most significant development on the American political landscape during the intervening years—insofar as the overall budgetary process is concerned—has been the rise of the "modern" or "institutionalized" presidency. The history of executive reform—as exemplified by the Brownlow Commission, the Reorganization Act of 1939, the establishment of the Executive Office of the President, the Hoover Commissions, etc.—has been adequately described elsewhere and need not delay us here except to note the pace and extent of its progress.[26]

In contrast, reform of congressional budget procedures has lagged far behind. Congressional hopes for GAO participation in the budget process, reaffirmed in the Legislative Reorganization Act of 1946, have been disappointed—not to mention the expectations for the legislative budget. The net effect has been a marked increase in leverage for the President in the budget process, through the effective development of his role of budget formulation. This may be an inevitable product of the explicit transfer of this role from the Congress to the executive (although it could be argued that no one was performing the role in the late nineteenth century).[27] Yet, if one reads the intent of Congress as it has been suggested here, the answer lies less in a willing acquiescence to executive leadership than in an inability to produce requisite congressional reforms. Which returns us to the major concern of this paper.

To summarize the discussion to this point, the reforms of 1921 appear to have been a watershed in

---

[26] For a general discussion of executive reform see Clinton Rossiter, *The American Presidency* (rev. ed.; New York: Harcourt, Brace & World, 1960), chap. iv, "The Modern Presidency." See also Richard E. Neustadt, "Presidency and Legislation: The Growth of Central Clearance," *American Political Science Review,* September 1954, pp. 641-71, and "Presidency and Legislation: Planning the President's Program," *American Political Science Review,* December 1955, pp. 980-1021.

[27] William H. Riker argues that "legislative government" cannot endure a budget. Before 1921, the United States Government worked without one. But when budgeting was introduced it transferred financial control to the budget maker. Thus today "real initiative in appropriations is in the President." See his discussion of the executive power in *Democracy in the United States* (New York: Macmillan, 1953), pp. 203-19.

the development of the contemporary roles of the legislature and executive in the budgetary process. The fixing of responsibility in the executive for the formulation of the budget was one of the key elements in the development of the modern presidency. Congress, much more reluctant to reform its basic appropriation function, has not yet developed the full potential of its roles in the budgetary process for reasons to be analyzed.

Major Characteristics of the Congressional Budget Process

In its broadest definition the congressional budget process has five major functional dimensions: authorization, appropriation, revenue legislation, economic analysis (and coordination of economic policy), and expenditure review (see Figure II). Most of the literature on congressional consideration of the budget is limited to the first two or three of these functions. This reflects the emphasis of Congress itself, as well as the newness of the Joint Economic Committee mechanism and the chronic disinclination of Congress to develop the function of expenditure review.[28]

The distinction between authorization and appropriation is basic to the congressional budget system; it is one of the major organizational principles of the Congress itself. Since 1837 the rules of the House of Representatives have forbidden appropriations for any expenditure not previously authorized by law. The rules also prohibit general legislation (the province of the "legislative" or "authorizing" committees such as Agriculture, Armed Services, Banking and Currency, etc.) in appropriation bills. In theory each of the two houses has been organized on the dual basis of legislative committees as distinct from *the* appropriations committee—leaving to one side the investigating and housekeeping committees. Appropriations Committees of the House and Senate have been organized on the basis of largely autonomous subcommittees which roughly parallel the legislative committees in structure. (Both tend to reflect the departmental structure of the federal bureaucracy.) The function of the legislative committees is to review, as the agent of the House or Senate, substantive policy questions within jurisdictions defined by the rules of the respective houses.[29] Legislation authorizing the expenditure of funds

---

[28] Smithies, *op. cit.,* pp. 65, 154.

[29] Arthur W. Macmahon, "Congressional Oversight of Administration: The Power of the Purse: I," *Political Science Quarterly,* June 1943, p. 173, includes under authorization "the passage of acts which define purposes, convey power, and authorize appropriations."

for agency programs is reported from these committees.] Authorization sets the *effective ceiling* for the congressional budget process.[30] Authorizations may be open-ended, requiring no further action by the legislative committee; they may be multi-year or lump sum, expiring when either the time or expenditure limitation is exceeded; or they may be annual—i.e., requiring action by the legislative committee concerned *each* fiscal year. The assumption underlying the specialized legislative committees is that they will be in a position to develop a full understanding of their subject-matter jurisdiction and to advise the Congress on substantive policy questions. They are to recommend the policy guidelines for congressional action.]

The function of the Appropriations Committee of each House is, in theory, subordinate to functions of the legislative committees and to congressional authorization. A clear distinction is drawn between making policy and appropriating funds to implement policy. Legislative provisions in appropriation bills may be ruled out of order on the floor.[31] The function of an appropriations committee is merely to weigh the various requests for funds in terms

of the fiscal requirements of the situation and to make the most efficient and economical allocation of funds to objects previously authorized. Appropriation bills must wait prior authorization before they can be reported for floor consideration, although certain appropriations may have permanent authorization. (See Figure III for a schematic representation of tne relation of the congressional authorization - appropriations processes.) The assumption is that the Appropriations Committee, while coordinating control of the purse, does not have the proper orientation or grounding for substantive policy decisions.

To students of public administration, the difficulties of this distinction are immediately obvious. To say that the appropriation of money is not making policy is tantamount to saying that budgeting is a nonpolitical activity. Congress through its legislative committees may determine the objects of expenditure and upper limits of funding, but the Appropriations Committee has the task of setting priorities among competing objects and determining the extent of funding. There is no clear-cut boundary line between the authorizing and appropriating com-

---

[30] When authorization acts carry language authorizing such amounts as may be necessary to be appropriated, the final determination is made in the appropriation act.

[31] However, the Appropriations Committee can and frequently does request a rule from the Rules Committee waiving all points of order. See James A. Robinson, *The House Rules Committee* (Indianapolis: Bobbs-Merrill, 1963), pp. 47-51.

mittees. In some instances the relevant appropriations subcommittee effectively makes policy. In others it makes few changes in the recommendations of the substantive committee. In still other cases basic legislation may determine the actual level of appropriations.[32]

In effect there are two separate structures of power existing in parallel within each house. The division of labor between authorization and appropriation produces an inescapable tension within the congressional system—the recognition of which is crucial to an understanding of congressional behavior in the budgetary sphere. This has been implicit in our historical analysis of the budget process. Between 1876 and 1885

the appropriations structure of power eclipsed the legislative committees, until the House revolted and went to the opposite extreme by dividing the appropriations function among the major legislative committees. The effect on fiscal control was disastrous. Then 1920 brought the compromise solution of a unified Appropriations Committee with circumscribed powers. With the advent of major expenditure programs in the 1940's and 1950's (such as defense, foreign aid, and space) there was some accretion of power to the appropriations committees, but this has been counterbalanced by the recent trend toward annual and multi-year authorization.[33] We shall return to the problems this

---

[32] For a discussion of the policy role of the appropriation subcommittees in foreign policy see Holbert N. Carroll, *The House of Representatives and Foreign Affairs* (University of Pittsburgh Press, 1958), pp. 139-93. Smithies, *op. cit.,* pp. 175-78, discusses the problem of authorizations determining appropriations, especially through open-ended programs providing specific rates of payment.

[33] Resentment toward Appropriations was expressed by one congressman as follows: "Theoretically the weapons system is authorized by the Committee on Armed Services, but that is only in theory. On the missile programs that have been permitted to go ahead, decision is made by the Appropriations Committee through the language of reports and through riders. The committee which heard all the testimony and is presumed to have special competence is not the one which makes the decision." Cited in Charles L. Clapp, *The Congressman: His Work as He Sees It* (Washington: Brookings Institution, 1963), p. 220. Note also the reply to this statement by a second congressman: "Isn't it a fact that the Armed Services Committee doesn't really make decisions on major problems, that it involves itself more with housekeeping and peripheral matters? I suspect that if we had an Armed Services Committee that made substantial policy decisions rather than accommodations between weapons systems, then the Appropriations Committee would not be in a position to do what it now does." *Ibid.* For an interesting account of the move toward annual authorization and in the defense area, see Raymond H. Dawson, "Congressional Innovation and Intervention in Defense Policy: Legislative Authorization of Weapons Systems," *American Political Science Review,* March 1962, pp. 42-57. An account of the fight for annual authorization of the space program is included in Alton Frye and John S. Saloma, "Congress and Science Policy: the Struggle to Participate" (Unpublished Paper, July 1963).

duality of structure imposes on the budgetary process later. It should be noted in passing that authorization-appropriations duality in the Senate is moderated by overlapping membership on committees and by the orientation of the Senate Committee on Appropriations which is less inclined toward budget cutting than the House Committee.

A second characteristic of the congressional budget process, more general than the duality of authorization-appropriation, is the decentralization of decision making. This is reflected both in the division of labor and specialization of function and in the norm of "reciprocity." The interrelationship of these norms —specialization and reciprocity—as an integrative force in decision making has been illustrated in the case of the House Appropriations Committee and its subcommittees by Richard Fenno:

> Conflict . . . is minimized by the deference traditionally accorded to the recommendation of the subcommittee which has specialized in the area, has worked hard,

and has "the facts." "It's a matter of 'You respect my work and I'll respect yours!' " It's frowned upon if you offer an amendment in the full Committee if you aren't on the subcommittee. It's considered presumptious to pose as an expert if you aren't on the subcommittee.[34]

These norms appear to operate generally throughout the congressional system, although to a lesser extent in the Senate.[35] They help to explain how the system, in spite of the fragmentation of functions to a variety of units, manages to effect action.[36] They extend from the House and Senate to their committees, from one committee to another, from the full committee to the relevant subcommittee, from subcommittee to subcommittee, and from member to member.

The decentralization of decision making in the congressional budget system would appear to be an inevitable consequence of the need for Congress to resolve itself into smaller units capable of acquiring specialized knowledge on a wide range of subjects. The standing com-

[34] Fenno, *loc. cit.*, p. 316.

[35] See Donald R. Mathews, *U.S. Senators and Their World* (Raleigh: University of North Carolina Press, 1960), chap. v, "Folkways of the Senate"; also John W. Baker (ed.), *Member of the House: Letters of a Congressman by Clem Miller* (New York: Scribners, 1962); "The traditional deference to the authority of one of its committees overwhelms the main body. The whole fabric of Congress is based on committee expertness, and the practice of 'rewriting a bill on the floor' is thought of as bad business." p. 51.

[36] A summary of the major units in the congressional budget system and their functions is given in Figure II.

mittee system has been the basic element in the congressional power structure since at least 1825 and is likely to remain so short of a major redefinition of the role of Congress in the American system.[37] There are legitimate questions to be answered concerning the nature of committee participation in decision making, the relation of committees to the full legislature, and the coordination of committee actions. But criticisms of the decentralized committee system itself reveal either a basic misunderstanding of the functioning of Congress or more likely a dissatisfaction with the fact of congressional participation in decision making in the first place. The major functional components of the congressional budget process are divided among numerous committees, yet it is a basic assumption of this analysis that reform of the process—including greater coordination or amalgamation of the units performing these functions—must begin with an appreciation of the realities of power in the congressional standing committee system.

The final characteristic of the congressional budget process to be discussed here is what Aaron Wildavsky has described as the pattern of "reciprocal expectations" concern-

ing the roles and strategies of the major participants.[38] For the sake of simplicity the participants may be described as being limited to the agencies, the Bureau of the Budget, the House Appropriations Committee, and the Senate Appropriations Committee. In this four-actor system the following roles are accepted as natural and inevitable. The agency plays the advocate role with a vested interest in increased appropriations. It brings desirable programs to the attention of the Budget Bureau and the congressional committees, which fulfill the request-screening counter role. In fulfilling the advocate role, agencies resort to a variety of budgetary strategies to *defend* their base by guarding against cuts, to *increase* the size of their base by moving ahead with old programs, and to *expand* their base by adding new programs.[39] Agencies are expected to believe in the inherent worth of their programs and to make the best case possible for them. However, the strategies adopted in "the budget game," as we might describe it, soon leave the merits of the case and political considerations become dominant. Agency behavior may assume Machiavellian, or more precisely,

---

[37] See Galloway, *op. cit.,* chap. vi, "Development of Committee System."
[38] See "Political Implications of Budgetary Reform," *Public Administration Review,* Autumn 1961, pp. 183-90. Also *The Politics of the Budgetary Process, op. cit.,* pp. 160-65.
[39] See Wildavsky's discussion of agency strategies, *ibid.,* pp. 18-35.

Parkinsonian aspects. One interesting example is the "both ends against the middle" strategy of playing off the authorization vs. the appropriations committees. A program is sold to the authorizing committee on the basis that the appropriations committee will screen the request and set the appropriations level, i.e., that there is no specific commitment. However, when the agency comes before the appropriations committee it will point to the authorization as a commitment for funds.

The Budget Bureau occupies a somewhat more ambiguous role in the process. Formally it screens agency requests and formulates the executive budget in accord with "the program of the President." In effect it establishes a starting point —an agenda for congressional consideration of the budget, a role that Congress could assume only with a heavy investment of time and staff resources. But by occupying a point at midstream in the budget process the Bureau is beset by a three-way conflict of interest in implementing its role. It is first of all agent and servant of the President and seeks in this capacity to impose some conception of national interest or priorities in expenditure on the total budget picture. This usually means cutting back agency estimates, although to varying degrees. Yet the Bureau does not have the authority to set appropriations—Congress remains the ultimate formal arbiter in the process. The agencies know this and are conscious of the need to cultivate political support and lines of access to the Congress and the relevant committees. One of the costs of the separation of powers in the federal budget process is this potential for dual loyalty. The Budget Bureau must therefore seek the confidence of the agencies—and this may frequently mean siding with the agency in developing a joint strategy toward the appropriations committees.[40] A reconciliation of agency advocacy and presidential interest may be possible through skillful negotiation and compromise but the net effect is agency-Bureau advocacy before the Congress. We have seen that the congressional interest in

---

[40] Wildavsky reaches a different conclusion: "Everyone knows that agencies make end-runs around the Bureau to gather support from Congress. If this happens too often, the Bureau finds that its currency is depreciated. Hence the Bureau frequently accepts consistent congressional action as a guide." *Ibid.*, p. 44. The utility of a joint strategy is minimized. Another interpretation is suggested by S. H. Huntington, *The Common Defense: Strategic Programs in National Politics* (New York: Columbia University Press, 1961). The budgetary process within the executive bureaucracy assumes some of the characteristics one usually associates with the legislative process—interagency and interbureau bargaining, negotiation, and compromise. Thus, when the President presents his budget, the Budget Bureau assumes an essentially defensive posture, treating budgetary decisions already reached as final, unwilling to upset the set of balances achieved.

establishing the Budget Bureau was to help keep the agencies under control. Close cooperation between the Bureau and the appropriations committees was anticipated as evidenced by section 212 of the 1921 Act which required the Bureau to furnish any committee having jurisdiction over revenue or appropriations "such aid and information as it may request." Subsequent friction only further illustrates the difficulty of the Bureau's position in the process.[41]

In this pattern of reciprocal expectations, the role of the House Committee on Appropriations is to effect a counter-role to the advocacy of the agencies and the quasi-advocacy of the Budget Bureau. Fenno has described this role in the essentially negative terms of "guardianship" of the Federal Treasury.[42] The vocabulary of action verbs most frequently used by members underlines this self image of the Committee— "cut," "carve," "slice," "prune," "whittle," "squeeze," "wring," "trim," "lop off," "chop," "slash," "pare," "shave," "fry," and "whack." The image has justification. With some notable exceptions the subcommittees of House Appropriations afford the most serious

hurdles in the budget process. The low point in the budget game—in the bidding and asking of the various plays—is usually the action taken by House Appropriations on the given budget request. That such a role should be played by someone in the system should be fairly obvious. Constitutionally and by subsequent decisions of the Congress this role has been vested with the House Committee on Appropriations. A basic change in the role of the committee presupposes a major reallocation of roles in the budget process—an approach that falls beyond the stated scope of this study. However, the manner in which this role is implemented is a legitimate subject for further discussion.

The last actor in this four-part game is the Senate Committee on Appropriations—a product of the bicameral organization of Congress. However, rather than provide a detailed review of the work of "the other body"—the normal justification for bicameralism—the Senate Committee has become a quasi-judicial "court of appeals" to which the agencies and Budget Bureau resort after undergoing the knife or meat-axe of the House Committee.

[41] See Arthur W. Macmahon, "Congressional Oversight of Administration: The Power of the Purse: II," *Political Science Quarterly,* September 1943, esp. pp. 407-14 for a discussion of the relations between the Bureau and the appropriations committees.

[42] Fenno, *loc. cit.,* pp. 311-12.

(The House Committee may also serve in this appellate capacity through consideration of supplemental appropriations. In any event, the final appeal is decided by the Congress as a whole.) In the budget game the Senate usually raises appropriations, the difference being settled in conference. Senate "extravagance" is a constant complaint of House members.[43]

Recently the Senate Committee, in a growing rivalry between the appropriations committees, has insisted on the right to initiate consideration of appropriations bills.[44] This would lead to a mixing of roles with attendant problems for other players in the game. Wildavsky concludes that such a development is unlikely however:

> The Senators value their ability to disagree on items in dispute as a means of maintaining their influence in crucial areas while putting the least possible strain on their time and energy.[45]

---

[43] Chairman Cannon's views are typical in this regard. "It would be a consummation devoutly to be wished if the other body would cooperate more closely . . . by resisting the importunities of the departments. . . . The Founding Fathers envisioned extravagant allowances in the House and armed the Senate with the amendment power to diminish it. How astonished they would be to note today how drastically the process has been reversed." *Congressional Record*, 88th Congress, 1st Session, December 30, 1963, p. 24370.

[44] See Senate, Committee on Government Operations, "Authority of the Senate to originate appropriations bills," Staff Memorandum No. 88-1-27, printed as an Appendix to *Hearings on S.537, Create a Joint Committee on the Budget*, 88th Congress, 1st Session, 1963, pp. 81-114. During the 88th Congress, 1st Session, the Senate Appropriations Committee had completed regular hearings on all items in several appropriation bills *prior to* their having been reported to the House of Representatives by the House Committee on Appropriations. In at least two instances no further hearings were held in the Senate Committee after House passage of the bills.

[45] Wildavsky, *op. cit.*, p. 52.

II.

COMMON CRITICISMS OF THE CONGRESSIONAL BUDGET PROCESS

Criticisms of the congressional budget process are about as varied and contradictory as criticisms of Congress itself. Congress pays too much attention to detail, not enough to broad policy. Lack of adequate congressional staff to dig into the details of agency budget estimates means that Congress appropriates in the dark. The authorization-appropriations "double" re-view leads to delays in the system and creates major administrative problems for the agencies. Congress has lost control of the budget and one of the chief villains is the authorizing committee. Thus run the criticisms. The extent of criticism should not come as a surprise, given the fact that fiscal reform occupies a prominent place on any agenda of congressional reform.

Behind each of these criticisms lies some normative assumption or objective in the budget process. Thus we should expect the criticisms to be shaped in terms of the positions and perspective of the actor or observer as well as by his political goals in the system. The assumption is made at the outset that budgeting in the American system is essentially a *political* activity. As Wildavsky has observed, "the crucial aspect of budgeting is whose preferences are to prevail in disputes about which activities are to be carried on and to what degree, in the light of limited resources."[1] However, the assumptions and objectives of the reformers—of all stripes—have never been as articulate or explicit as their criticisms. This may be explained by the fact that actors in the system may have a clear idea of what they dislike, but may be far less sure about what can be done to remedy the situation. It may also reflect a tendency of individuals, immersed in the day-to-day functioning of the system, to answer such questions from an intuitive or pragmatic approach rather than through a logical, rational theory of action. It may betray per-

spectives—e x e c u t i v e , legislative, committee, etc. — so deeply ingrained that the actors have never thought to articulate them. Finally, the possibility that some reformers may deliberately mask or falsely advertise their objectives to enhance probability of success should not be excluded.

This analysis proceeds from the stated criticisms of the congressional budget process, and some recent unsuccessful efforts to reform it, to a consideration of the objectives of reform. The purpose of this approach is to derive or define the major relevant values or goals of the participants prior to a consideration of actual reforms.

*   *   *   *   *

The major criticisms of the congressional budget process can be grouped under several subheadings: Each group of criticisms is summarized and discussed in turn:

1. *Congress has used the budget to control executive discretion in administration* rather than as an instrument for weighing expenditures versus revenues and allocating scarce resources. The appropriations act has become a device of

---

[1] "Political Implications of Budgetary Reform," *loc. cit.,* pp. 184-85. "Since the budget represents conflicts over whose preferences shall prevail . . . one cannot speak of 'better budgeting' without considering who benefits and who loses or demonstrating that no one loses. Just as the supposedly objective criterion of 'efficiency' has been shown to have normative implications, so a 'better budget' may well be a cloak for hidden policy preferences."

administrative management. Related criticisms are that Congress becomes bogged down in details of administration (which it is argued are not its province) and ignores the broad policy issues involved. Administrative control is also criticized for discouraging the very efficiency it seeks to achieve. Highly specific appropriations — a traditional weapon of control—restrict the discretion of administrative officials and remove incentives for initiative and improved efficiency. According to the critics this behavior of Congress is rooted in the assumption that the executive is "basically irresponsible" and that close congressional surveillance and control is essential.[2]

Comment. The criticisms all have some validity as a review of the historical record or of recent research into congressional "oversight" or surveillance indicate.[3] There is little disagreement as to the congressional intent of administrative control. Calhoun spoke for congressmen of every period when he argued in 1817 that the congressional power to raise and apply money was "the sinew of our strength"; that "not a cent of money ought to be applied, but by our direction, and under our control."[4] There is some disagreement concerning the fact of control. Some congressmen see it as ineffective or nonexistent. Conversely, some administrators may feel it to be oppressively real. The real disagreement, however, comes in the realm of political values and goals. One could define a continuum between pure executive discretion and total congressional direction, with the corresponding values of efficiency, decision, or "government" on the one hand and "representation" on the other.[5] An important conclusion suggested by

[2] Smithies, *op. cit.,* p. 167. This observation was made by the Taft Commission on Economy and Efficiency: "As a result of established legislative policy the Government is thereby robbed to an extent of the benefit of well trained technical service and of the exercise of official discretion—this on the theory that its officers are not to be trusted with the use of public funds, and therefore not to be held responsible for the exercise of judgment in the execution of the details of business." Cited in Wilmerding, *op. cit.,* p. 150.

[3] This is the thrust of Lucius Wilmerding's discussion of "the effort to control before expenditure." Systematic studies of various techniques of control and oversight have been undertaken by the Harvard Research Seminar: Congressional Supervision of Public Policy and Administration. See also Joseph Harris, *Congressional Control of Administration* (Washington: The Brookings Institution, 1964).

[4] Cited in Wilmerding, *op. cit.,* p. 81.

[5] The tension between these values is the theme of Theodore Lowi's *Congress and the Forces that Shape It: Legislative Politics U.S.A.* (Boston: Little, Brown & Co., 1962). See the editor's introduction, "Representation and Decision."

this disagreement is that the congressional budget process may serve *several* goals. To criticize Congress for not limiting itself to rational budgetary procedures thus appears highly unrealistic and simplistic.

But beyond this, the use of the budget as a means for congressional oversight can be defended on at least two more counts. First, in our preceding discussion of the reciprocal expectations of actors in the appropriations process the agencies and, to a lesser extent, the Budget Bureau assumed a role of advocacy. Suspicion of executive behavior would thus appear to be built into the system—barring some major redefinition of roles. A second argument is the secular transformation of executive-legislative relations. With the development of the modern presidency, with the assumption by the President of the role of "chief legislator"—the initiating focus in the legislative process—with the trend toward delegated legislation, the congressional role in legislation has changed. Theodore Lowi has defined the major focus of Congress

in the "executive-centered" government as "no longer simply that of prescribing the behavior of citizens but more often that of *affecting the behavior of administrators.*"[6]

In summary, the first group of criticisms describes one aspect of congressional behavior which may be evaluated favorably or unfavorably from different perspectives. Further comment is deferred until more of the picture is complete.

2. *Congress introduces centrifugal, particularistic, and local forces into the budgetary process,* thereby disrupting the rationality of the executive budget. According to this criticism Congress is not equipped to develop national plans, for example in resource development and allocation, and has therefore delegated this task to the executive. Congress then proceeds to short circuit the President by dealing directly with the executive agencies and local interests.[7] Recent attacks on the congressional pork barrel have focused on congressional solicitation of local interests.[8] A variant of this criticism is that individual

[6] *Ibid.*, p. xix. "In an executive-centered world it is not only the administrator but also Congress whose job is continuous. Thus more than ever congressional government is government by committees and subcommittees. . . . Now these committees are almost exclusive agents of continuing congressional supervision ('oversight') and clarification of law: the new forms of congressional power."

[7] See Arthur Maass, "Congress and Water Resources," *American Political Science Review,* September 1950, pp. 576-93; also "The Kings River Project" in Harold Stein, ed., *Public Administration and Policy Development: A Case Book* (The Inter-University Case Program; New York: Harcourt, Brace & Co., 1952), pp. 533-72.

[8] See "Now—See the Innards of a Fat Pig," *Life* Magazine, August 16, 1963. Also address by Edwin P. Neilan, National Press Club, Washington, August 7, 1963. For a

regions, industries, and local groups have become so dependent upon specific categories of federal expenditures that Congress has lost control of the budgetary process.[9]

Comment. Again the fact of such congressional behavior does not appear to be much in dispute although one can give examples of congressional action to counter centrifugal forces in the executive.[10] The disagreement is, then, on values. In this case the disagreement is more nearly between two concepts of representation: representation of the national interest through the presidential constituency, or representation of local interests (and derivatively the national interest) through the congressional constituency. We shall assume the continuation of a kind of dual representation or compromise between the two—and in the budget process a reasonable balance between centripetal and centrifugal forces.[11]

Even assuming this balance there remain unresolved problems: "reasonable" criteria in the award of local contracts and projects, the dependence of certain interests on budgetary subventions, and the control of new private interest demands on the Treasury. Again we cannot escape the fact that budgeting is a political activity and that congressmen are *par excellence* political men.

3. *The congressional budgetary process is irrational. It defies virtually all the precepts of "good budgeting."* Perhaps the most frequent and universal criticism of the congressional budgetary process is its lack of rationality and failure to correspond to any accepted theory of budgeting. The criticisms are legion: Congressional budgeting is

---

typical congressional response to the "pork-barrel" criticism see Congressman Kirwan's remarks, "Reclamation is Money in the Bank," *Congressional Record,* 88th Congress, 1st Session, August 14, 1963, pp. 14196-14200.

[9] See Murray L. Weidenbaum, *Federal Budgeting: The Choice of Government Programs* (Washington: American Enterprise Institute, 1964), esp. pp. 4-17, "The Pressures on Government Spending."

[10] Macmahon observes that Appropriations Committee reports are likely to include remarks that will later provide "fulcrums whereby the department can exercise leverage upon its self-assertive parts. . . . the pressures of the legislative body may be exerted in fortifying the central machinery within the administration itself." "Congressional Oversight of Administration . . . II," *loc cit.,* pp. 388-89.

[11] Smithies concludes that "a reasonable balance in the political system probably requires that centripetal influences should prevail with the Executive and centrifugal ones with the legislature." *Op. cit.,* p. 144. James MacGregor Burns, *Deadlock of Democracy: Four Party Politics in America* (Englewood Cliffs, N.J.: Prentice-Hall, 1963) feels that centrifugal forces need to be reduced. His proposals for restructuring party competition at the congressional level constitute, in effect, a merger of the congressional with the presidential constituency.

fragmented. Appropriations are not considered in relation to revenues. The budget is broken into segments with individual appropriation bills handled by virtually autonomous appropriations subcommittees. There is no formal coordination of these elements or of the related functions of expenditure review and assessing the economic consequences of the budget. The budget is not a comprehensive statement of federal expenditures and is thus deficient in one of the basic prerequisites for effective budgeting. The methods of congressional decision making on the budgetary questions have been especially subject to criticism. Congress becomes involved in administrative detail and fails to deal with basic policy issues (the other side of our first general criticism). Congressional budgeting is limited chiefly to incremental aspects—with the examination extending only to increases in estimates over budget allowances for the previous year: Consequently, comprehensive evaluations of the existing program bases, upon which the new requests rest, are bypassed. Congress prefers to handle the budget on a line-item rather than a program basis. Further related criticisms are that Congress makes budgetary decisions without adequate information and that it in-

dulges in capricious behavior by making sharp "meat-axe" cuts in the budget—later resorting to supplemental appropriations to restore deficiencies. To the economist trained in terms of marginal utility analysis in the allocation of scarce resources among competing projects, the congressional process is a sheer nightmare. The preoccupation of the literature with this general problem area reflects the extent of concern.[12]

Comment. Most of the proposals for budgetary reform have assumed the validity of this criticism. In fact, critics of the congressional process seem to delight in elaborating the irrationalities of the system and then reconstructing a rational whole. Budgeting is seen as a rational process, susceptible to the techniques of the economist — comprehensive means-ends analysis with allocation on the basis of some adaptation of the marginal utility formula. In extreme form these proposals assume the shape of a normative theory of budgeting, i.e., that it is possible to specify by means of the budget mechanism what the range and extent of governmental activities ought to be at a given time.

Recently, a second school of thought has challenged the assumptions of this approach to reform and

---

[12] See, for instance, Edward C. Banfield, "Congress and the Budget: A Planner's Criticism," *American Political Science Review*, December 1949, pp. 1217-28.

has attempted to discover a more subtle, if lower-order rationality in the congressional budget process.[13] The comprehensive approach to budgeting, it is argued, places too great a burden on man's limited ability to calculate. The possibility for a comprehensive means-ends analysis is further restricted when one realizes that "ends are rarely agreed upon, that they keep changing, that possible consequences of a single policy are too numerous to describe, and that knowledge of the chain consequences for other policies is but dimly perceived for most conceivable alternatives."[14] From this perspective, i.e., the need for Congress and individual congressmen to reduce the burden of calculation, much congressional behavior assumes a new rationality. Decentralization of decision making and the associated norms of specialization and reciprocity have already been described as essential to the functioning of Congress. Within the framework of reciprocal roles in the budget process, the incremental approach of the appropriations subcommittees, and the "meat-axe" reduction (subject to appeal and supplemental appropriations) afford major aids for calculating budgets.[15]

The rebuttal to a normative theory of budgeting has been useful. It has reemphasized the political assumptions behind the economics of resource allocation. It has questioned the validity of a completely rational approach and has called attention to hidden rationalities in the congressional system. Yet it runs the risk—as does any protest movement—of overstating its case. "What is" tends to become what "ought to be."[16] To point out the limits of rationality is not sufficient cause to answer the demands for greater rationality in

[13] Aaron Wildavsky draws upon Charles Lindblom's more general analysis in "The Science of Muddling Through," *Public Administration Review,* Spring 1959, pp. 79-88. See his further references.

[14] Wildavsky, "Budgetary Calculations and Budgetary Strategies," Paper presented at the Annual Meeting of the American Political Science Association, Washington, September 1962, p. 8.

[15] Smithies also sees value in the "meat-axe" approach *but* because it is in his view a necessary counterpart of executive discretion. The "scalpel" approach implies highly specific appropriations. *Op. cit.,* p. 146. Huitt lists a number of techniques which have all "the common characteristic of requiring little information and little exercise of decision," *loc. cit.,* p. 440.

[16] See for instance the conclusion to Wildavsky's *Politics of the Budgetary Process,* p. 178. ". . . James Buchanan has observed 'To argue that an existing order is "imperfect" in comparison with an alternative that turns out, upon careful inspection, to be unobtainable, may not be different from arguing that the existing order is "perfect." ' A basic conclusion of this appraisal is that the existing budgetary process works much better than is commonly supposed."

the system. The task of the reformer is instead to reorder his assumptions as to the nature of the congressional budget process and to make new proposals accordingly. But this anticipates the argument of the paper.

In summary, the irrationality of the congressional budgetary process remains perhaps its major criticism. However, proposals for reform cannot limit themselves to purely economic requirements of budget theory. A basic limitation to the "rationalization" of the congressional system remains the requirement of decentralization for specialization. With these warnings there would still appear to be room for enhancing the rationality of congressional decisions.

3a. *The congressional budgetary process is INTENTIONALLY irrational.* Congress prefers to behave irresponsibly in dealing with fiscal matters. Congress prefers confusion.[17] . Congress deliberately obfuscates (or refuses to clarify) its action in the budgetary process in order to mask intrusions upon the executive budget.

Comment. This sub-criticism develops the previous criticism in terms of congressional intent, and is accordingly a more serious charge. In fairness one should note the counter evidence—the continued efforts on the part of Congress to achieve greater internal rationality: the reforms of 1920-21, the legislative budget, the consolidated appropriations bill, the proposed Joint Committee on the Budget, etc. The failure to achieve these reforms cannot be explained simply as congressional duplicity. The full range of causes must first be examined. No doubt, elements within Congress benefit from the irrationalities or idiosyncracies of present arrangements, and these interests are unlikely to acquiesce to reforms that reduce their power or access. Yet this is not equivalent to saying that Congress condones such action or that Congress could not or has not acted to override such interests.

4. *Congress lacks or has lost control of federal spending through its authorization-appropriations process.* The federal budget has increased to a size where it is out of effective control. This has led to deficit financing and a mounting national debt—i.e., fiscal irresponsibility. Congress, it is argued, must share part of the blame for this state of affairs. It has not exercised an effective check at the authorizing stage. It has paid little attention to the time dimension of expenditures. Special interests mount campaigns and win congressional support for new programs. These decisions are

---

[17] This is a "disquieting" conclusion reached by Holbert Carroll, *op. cit.,* pp. 207-08.

cumulative and become built-in rigidities in the budgets of succeeding years. Thus the budget in a given year largely represents prior commitments. Murray Weidenbaum in a study of the 1964 budget concluded that only 58 percent of the budget was subject to effective review, and if one excluded the security-related agencies the figure dropped to 23 percent.[18] Related criticisms include the failure to make the budget comprehensive, the failure to eliminate routes for bypassing the appropriations committees such as backdoor financing, and the spending tendency of the legislative committees versus the appropriations committees.

Comment. This set of criticisms would appear to be supported by budgetary data and expressed dissatisfaction within Congress itself. Our previous discussion of the tension between the parallel structures of legislative and appropriations committees is also suggestive. The late Clarence Cannon's diagnosis that Congress lacks the will to say "no" is one possible explanation. The irrationality and complexity of the system, however, would impose problems regardless of congressional will. There is also the question of adequacy of informational inputs to the system. Regardless of the explanation, the breakdown of control is a central concern to reform of the budgetary system.

5. *The congressional budget system receives inadequate informational inputs to function effectively.* This criticism has several components. First it is argued that Congress does not obtain independent, objective information. The agencies and Budget Bureau, the sources of most of its information, are advocates of agency and presidential interests—and cannot be impartial. Congress, on the other hand, has failed to equip itself with adequate staff for this purpose. Secondly there is the related question of the information requirements of the system. Congress, it is said, receives too much, not too little information. It needs to evaluate and digest information that will be useful to the performance of its functions. Under the current system Congress appropriates blindly. Congress has no way of knowing the effects of its budgetary actions on the executive agencies.[19] Thirdly there is the question of distribution of information among committees and individual members. Some critics

---

[18] Weidenbaum, *op. cit.,* pp. 39ff.

[19] This is Wallace's major criticism of congressional "control" of federal spending. Congress does not exercise its constitutional power over expenditures with knowledge and understanding of the consequences of its action. *Op. cit.,* pp. 3-17.

note a tendency of committees to "closet" or "squirrel" information as a form of power. The behavior of the House Appropriations Committee has been cited in this regard.[20] The effect of maldistribution of information is both to reduce the effectiveness of whatever informal coordination may exist between the units of the system and to increase the sense of frustration and inefficacy of the individual member. Lastly there remains the question of the use of information. Even if Congress has a full range of informational inputs and even if all information has perfect distribution, will the elements of the decision-making structure use it? Or will the committee chairman overrule the advice of his staff or simply disregard available information in reaching his decision?

· *Comment.* Again on the basis of continued expressed dissatisfaction within Congress, the adequacy of informational inputs and distribution would appear to be a legitimate area for criticism. Some of this dissatisfaction, however, may well be with the decision-making system it-self and with the power of units like House Appropriations. Information and the request for it may become just another aspect of the jurisdictional struggle among committees. Even under an assumption of complete information within the system, it is not clear what, if any, changes there would be in the outcome of decisions. The legislative process adds by definition political (value) judgments and considerations of power-brokerage or bargaining to budgetary solutions. The problem may then be to define limits to the non-use of information —i.e., how irrational the system can or should be in its allocation decisions.

6. *The congressional budget process does not accommodate the functioning of explicit majority-minority party roles.* Congressional budgetary machinery minimizes the expression of partisanship. Party leadership committees have no systematic role in the consideration of the budget. If Congress is ever to operate on the model of a "responsible two-party system," party roles, it is argued, must be defined in the

---

[20] Fenno's analysis of the norms underlying the power of House Appropriations suggests the importance of the tradition against minority reports in the subcommittee and full committee—an effective means for screening information. *Loc. cit.,* pp. 316-18. One member of the House interviewed in relation to this study remarked, "One way to be an expert is to keep others ignorant." Robert Wallace, *op. cit.,* pp. 173-74, suggests that the appropriations committees have discouraged the development of GAO studies. ". . . If there is another source of information, their power is considerably diffused and their judgment not so vital."

budgetary process.[21]

Comment. Two factors may explain this observation of nonpartisanship. First, the differentiation of executive and legislative roles in the budgetary process has predominated over majority and minority roles within Congress. The former remain fairly stable over a given period of time; the latter fluctuate, depending upon which party happens to occupy the presidency and control the Senate and/or House. The greatest need for an explicit minority role in the congressional system is when the majority party controls both the executive and legislature. The majority suffers from a conflict of interest that may bar it as an impartial critic of the President's program.[22]

Secondly, nonpartisanship as an operating norm is a prerequisite for committee "integration" and integration is one of the primary determinants of committee power.[23] It follows that powerful elements in the system, such as House Appropriations, will discourage open partisan divisions in order to preserve their power. However, the case just noted, of a majority party in total control, appears to have produced counter-pressures for a minority role. The creation of the "Bow" Task Force of House Republican members of the Appropriations Committee and its concerted efforts —in cooperation with the minority leadership—to cut the President's budget is an important exception to the observed nonpartisan behavior of the system.[24]

7. *Congressional consideration of*

[21] See Smithies, *op. cit.*, pp. 192-97. "The expression of majority and minority views . . . would tend to center debate on real issues rather than on the superstitions and phantoms that so often becloud budgetary discussion." For a general statement on the need for a responsible two-party system see Commission on Political Parties of the American Political Science Association, "Toward a More Responsible Two-Party System," *American Political Science Review*, Pt. II, supplement September 1950, pp. 15-36.

[22] *The Congressional Quarterly*, Weekly Report No. 9, March 1, 1963, p. 240, provides an illustration of this problem: "House Speaker John W. McCormack (D Mass.) Feb. 20 told reporters that many senior Republicans . . . were satisfied with current staffing arrangements. He said he knew that the so-called Republican 'activists' like Ford, Schwengel, Griffin, Curtis, and Peter Frelinghuysen Jr. (N.J.) were trying to develop independent Republican programs but that he saw no need for this since the job of the Democratic Congress was to enact the President's program and the 'activist' movement might be detrimental by creating delays."

[23] This is a conclusion of two studies of "powerful" committees: Fenno's study of House Appropriations (*loc. cit.*, pp. 323-24) and the Green and Rosenthal study of the Joint Committee on Atomic Energy. See Harold P. Green and Alan Rosenthal, *Government of the Atom: The Integration of Powers* (New York: Atherton Press, 1963), pp. 44-65.

[24] See "Economy Drive Progressing," *Congressional Record*, 88th Congress, 1st Session, December 9, 1963, pp. 22768-74. Congressman Pillion observed "For the first

the budget is unduly lengthy and disrupts agency planning and efficiency in operations. Congress has enacted continuing resolutions, deferring final action on appropriations bills several months into the new fiscal year. The trend toward annual authorization has increased the problem of delay in appropriations. Agencies are held at the operating level of continuing resolutions regardless of their needs for the new fiscal year. Congress, it is argued, loses public esteem by reason of its inordinate delays in appropriating funds.[25]

Comment. The subject of delays in the congressional budget process is not a new point of criticism. However, congressional performance in the last two sessions of Congress (Eighty-seventh: second, and Eighty-eighth: first) has caused a new level of concern. In reply, the late Appropriations chairman, Clarence Cannon, pointed to the savings achieved by the continuing resolutions and extended congressional review.[26] He also placed the blame for delay in appropriations bills on the authorizing committees.[27] Other factors, however, have contributed to the delays. The dispute over prerogatives between the House and Senate Appropriations Committees virtually paralyzed the appropriations process at the conference stage during the Eighty-seventh Congress.[28] The Civil Rights bill reportedly caused Southern committee chairmen to slow consideration of other legislation in order to enhance their bargaining position. The political aspects of scheduling were noted by several members and staff interviewed. "They are like card players holding tricks." "The leadership is just as guilty; they hold up action on appropriation bills to the end of the session so they can squeeze things through." "They're playing politics with the congressional system. We should abide by the spirit of the terminal date and

---

time in my memory, the Republican members of the Appropriations Subcommittees worked as a team with specific appropriation reduction targets." Congressman Bow announced that the task force would continue in the next session.

[25] See series of three feature articles on the delay in appropriations by Jerry Klutz and Carroll Kilpatrick, *The Washington Post*, September 15, 16, 17, 1963. See also "Congress Takes 12 Months to Clear Funds," *Congressional Quarterly Almanac*, 88th Congress, 1st Session (1963) pp. 132-34.

[26] *Congressional Record,* 88th Congress, 1st Session, September 12, 1963, pp. 16048-50. See also remarks of Congressman Pillion, *ibid.,* December 6, 1963, p. 22770.

[27] See section "Late enactment of the appropriation bills," *Congressional Record,* 88th Congress, 1st Session, December 30, 1963, pp. 24372-74.

[28] See "Senate-House Feud Stalls Appropriations," *Congressional Quarterly Almanac,* 87th Congress, 2d Session (1962), pp. 144-46.

stop playing politics with time."

The trend toward annual and multi-year authorizations has without question been a factor in the delays. Over $26 billion of the 1964 budget required annual reprocessing of legislative authorizations. However, the benefits gained need to be weighed against the obvious costs in loss of efficiency. In the area of defense policy, Raymond Dawson has suggested that the annual authorization procedure may enhance the role of congressional leaders in three regards: (1) it strengthens the *access* of Congress to the processes of policy formulation (it involves more congressmen in "the intellectual, technical and political processes from which policy and strategy emerge"), (2) it affords a *utility of focus* while defense appropriations must roam across an immense terrain of policy decisions, and (3) it creates an *expanded base of knowledge* in Congress for the critical analysis of defense issues.[29] Similar conclusions are indicated in the case of the annual authorization for the space program.[30]

Annual and multi-year authorizations have meant some reduction in power of the appropriations committee, not to mention the restrictions placed on scheduling. The lack of sympathy from this quarter should come as no surprise. Yet Congress, sensing the gains in this new technique of oversight, is expanding its application. The resultant delay in congressional scheduling is one of the unsolved problems of the congressional budgetary process.

* * * * *

Criticisms of the congressional budgetary system could be further elaborated. Some frequent criticisms—the failure to weigh appropriations and revenues, the erratic congressional performance in postaudit review, the inadequacies of congressional machinery for an overall review of national economic policy, etc. — have been treated briefly or indirectly as part of more general criticism. Instead, we have selected and commented upon a broad range of general criticisms. It should be obvious to the reader that the criticisms come from a variety of perspectives and that they are neither additive nor susceptible to a simple rank listing. In fact, what one viewer may consider a criticism another may see as an advantage of the system. Some of the underlying value considerations have been defined, others must await a more general analysis.

[29] Dawson, *loc. cit.*, pp. 56-57.
[30] Frye and Saloma, *op. cit.*, pp. 17-21, 27-28.

III.

CONGRESSIONAL INITIATIVE: MAJOR ATTEMPTS TO REFORM THE CONGRESSIONAL BUDGETARY SYSTEM

One major set of questions remains to be answered before we can consider a strategy for fiscal reform. Why has Congress failed to reform and develop its budgetary procedures in the face of extensive executive innovation? The result has been a differential development in legislative and executive roles defined in the reforms of 1921—with a marked increase in executive leverage. What efforts has Congress made at self-reform and why have these met with such limited success? Answers to these questions are essential to an intelligent discussion of reform proposals. Five important areas of congressional initiative are examined: congressional use of the General Accounting Office, increased staff for the appropriations committees, the legislative budget (the Joint Committee on the Legislative Budget established under the Legislative Reorganization Act of 1946), the Omnibus Appropriations bill, and the Joint Committee on the Budget (the McClellan Committee).

Congressional Utilization of the General Accounting Office

The GAO was created, as we have noted, as part of the budgetary reforms of 1921, both to assist Congress in the post-examination or review of budgetary expenditures and to serve as a counterweight to the Bureau of the Budget in the executive branch. The broad investigating and reporting authority vested in the GAO by section 312 of the Budget and Accounting Act en-

compassed both pre- and post-examination of the budget.[1] However, Congress has never developed a pre-audit budgetary role for the GAO. Even today the GAO does not see agency budget justifications until after the appropriations bills have been passed.[2] Congress avoided the question of a pre-audit budgetary role in the Legislative Reorganization Act of 1946. Section 206 of the Act, which "directed" the Comptroller General to make an "expenditure analysis" of each executive agency, including government corporations, sought only "to determine whether public funds have been economically and efficiently *administered* and *expended*" (my italics).[3] While the appropriations committees in reviewing

[1] See Testimony of Joseph Campbell, Comptroller General of the United States, Senate, Committee on Government Operations, *Hearings on S.537, op. cit.,* pp. 33-34. The Comptroller General testified that his office had done considerable work under section 312(b) of the Budget and Accounting Act, 1921, requiring the making of such investigations and reports as ordered by either House of Congress or by any committee of either House having jurisdiction over revenues, appropriations, or expenditures, and that on occasion this work had related to budget estimates.

[2] *Ibid,* p. 36. Comptroller General Campbell observed, "It is surprising and unfortunate that an organization such as ours, does not have access to the budget justification well before they reach you sometime in January each year. As a matter of fact, we do not usually see the budget justification until after the appropriation bills have been passed."

[3] The Joint Committee on the Organization of the Congress clearly had a business type "service audit" in mind. "Such a service audit should include reports on the administrative performance and broad operations of the agency, together with information that will enable Congress to determine whether public funds are being carelessly, extravagantly or loosely administered and spent. In most cases the present detailed audit of items does not reveal the general condition of the agency's operation." Joint Committee on the Organization of the Congress, *Report of: Organization of the Congress,* Senate Report. No. 1011, 79th Congress, 2d Session, 1946, p. 22. Robert Wallace, *op. cit.,* pp. 164-67, "Possibilities of Section 206," suggests a wide range of pre-audit GAO activities that are inherent in a full implementation of Section 206: sitting as

agency performance during appropriations hearings might use these expenditure analyses, the law was permissive.

Subsequent efforts to spell out the GAO role in this area have won wide support in Congress but have yet to be enacted into law. The House Committee on Government Operations reported favorably on several amendments to section 206 during the Eighty-fifth Congress. One provided for investigations and reports by the Comptroller General upon the request of the chairman of the House or Senate Appropriations Committee "to assist the committee in considering the items in the President's budget and the justification therefor."[4] The McClellan bill for a Joint Committee on the Budget, which has passed the Senate on several occasions, and the House Rules Committee once (the Colmer bill) would authorize the Comptroller General to make such investigations and reports as would enable the Joint Committee "to give adequate consideration to items . . . which

are contained in the budget as submitted by the President, and the justifications submitted in support thereof."[5]

Why has Congress failed to develop the full budgetary roles envisioned for the GAO in the 1921 reform legislation? The answers are instructive to the student of the legislative process—essential to any discussion of fiscal reform. Several explanations contribute to an understanding of congressional inaction:

1. *The adjustment of institutional roles.* The GAO might have been created *de novo* as a concept but it could not escape the fact that many of its functions had a Treasury background and many of its staff members were recruited from within the Treasury. The congressional committees on public expenditure had been reluctant to use the services of Treasury auditors and comptrollers during the nineteenth century because they did not trust their performance.[6] This attitude of distrust of "Treasury types"

observers during budget formulation, studying justification sheets, procuring information by subpoena, appearing at committee hearings to give testimony, etc. Section 312(b) of the 1921 Act would appear to be a better authority for these activities than Section 206 however.

[4] *Financial Management in the Federal Government, op. cit.,* p. 196.

[5] S.537 was proposed as an amendment to section 138 (legislative budget) of the Reorganization Act. Comptroller General Campbell testified that while section 312(b) of the Budgeting and Accounting Act of 1921 was broad enough to encompass such requests from the Joint Committee, the GAO thought it "desirable to spell out the specific authority in the law." *Hearings on S.537, op. cit.,* p. 34.

[6] Wilmerding, *op. cit.,* pp. 221-22.

carried over into the post-1921 period. The relevant congressional committees simply did not ask for the staff services of the GAO. The failure of GAO to adjust to the concept of the 1921 Act is also attributable in part to the agency's self image as developed under the first Comptroller General, J. Raymond McCarl (1921-36). McCarl saw his function as one of preventing fraud, illegal expenditures, or malpractice. He required that every voucher be examined in Washington by the GAO and used as his chief weapon his authority to disallow expenditures by executive officers. GAO operations became highly centralized and concerned primarily with the settlement of disbursement accounts.[7] By the time of the Legislative Reorganization Act, the GAO had not fully developed its post-audit role, let alone a budgetary pre-audit role. The comprehensive (commercial type) audit program was not adopted until

1949. It should be noted, however, that the GAO has revised its conception of its role under its current and past Comptroller Generals Joseph Campbell (1954-present) and Lindsay C. Warren (1940-54). In spite of the failure of Congress to appropriate money specifically for the implementation of expenditure analyses under section 206, the GAO has been shifting rapidly to comprehensive audits. It now makes over 1,500 examinations, audits, and reviews annually and submits over 300 reports each year to the Congress, as contrasted with relatively few as recently as 1944-45.[8]

2. *The unsuitability of a post-audit orientation to a budgetary pre-audit role.* Some critics of the GAO within and without Congress argue that the GAO—with its traditional emphasis on auditing to ensure compliance with the law rather than to promote program efficiency—is not equipped to perform a major new budgetary role.[9] They question

[7] See Gerald C. Schulsinger, *The General Accounting Office: Two Glimpses* (Inter-University Case Program: Cases in public administration, ICP case series, No. 35: University of Alabama, 1956).

[8] Performance of its responsibilities under section 206 is cited by GAO as one of the reasons for institution of its comprehensive audit program "to determine how well the agency or activity under audit is discharging its financial responsibilities." *GAO Policy and Procedure Manual for Guidance of Federal Agencies,* Title 2, section 2010. For a summary of GAO audit reports see General Accounting Office, *Annual Report of the Comptroller General of the United States for Fiscal Year 1963,* p. 1 and Appendix: "Audit reports issued by the General Accounting Office."

[9] This is the argument of Arthur Smithies: "While there is much to be said for the point of view that auditing is a legislative responsibility which should not be delegated, the suggestion [of providing audit reports to a Joint Congressional Committee] diverts attention from the major requirement: information that will enable the Congress to grapple with the problem of economy and efficiency. And this is not included in the current conception of auditing." *Op. cit.,* p. 156.

whether personnel with an auditing background can assume the role of a budget examiner, whether these skills do not require a different training, and whether the GAO would not have to recruit a new and separate staff to perform a pre-audit role. However, the GAO has already demonstrated some flexibility in this regard in the shift toward comprehensive audits. The McClellan bill has further moved to counter this argument by providing the Comptroller General with authority to employ technical and professional personnel without regard to civil service laws, rules, or regulations and to fix their compensation without regard to the Classification Act of 1949. This criticism of the GAO would appear to be more a description of the agency's past than an inherent attribute of the system.

3. *The congressional concern for economy in its own area of administration.* The ostensible reason for the failure to develop the GAO, especially expenditure analyses

under section 206, has been the unwillingness of Congress (notably the House Committee on Appropriations) to appropriate the necessary funds. The Comptroller General requested $1 million in the Independent Offices Appropriations Bill for fiscal year 1948 to begin implementing section 206. Subcommittee Chairman Wigglesworth denied the request on the grounds that committee staff had been increased under the Reorganization Act and that no additional staff was required by the GAO. The Comptroller General took the opposite view, but when subsequent requests for funds were also denied he announced that the GAO would carry out section 206 along with its other functions from its basic appropriation.[10] Taken by itself, this argument would appear to be a rather short-sighted economy. We shall see in due course that the House Committee on Appropriations has refused to enlarge its own staff for similar reasons. Former chairman

---

[10] *Financial Management in the Federal Government, op. cit.,* pp. 32-33, "Expenditure Analysis by the General Accounting Office"; also see testimony of Lindsay C. Warren, Comptroller General, Senate Committee on Expenditures in the Executive Departments, *Hearings on S.193,* 82d Congress, 1st Session, 1951, p. 149. The Comptroller General on December 6, 1946, by Office Order No. 67, Supplement No. 3 had assigned to the former Corporation Audits Division of GAO the duties necessary to accomplish the purposes of section 206 in the case of government corporations or other establishments audited by the Division. One staff member of the House Appropriations Committee observed in an interview that the GAO didn't need to ask for the funds specifically. "It was just an excuse for a big increase."

Cannon was reputed to hold the belief that economy started at home.[11]

4. *Legislative prerogative of the House Committee on Appropriations.* While an expanded budgetary role for the GAO should assist the Appropriations Committee in its review of the President's budget, the availability of GAO studies to a Joint Budget Committee, other committees, or the congressional membership would lessen the power of information now exercised by members of the appropriations committees. The House Committee on Appropriations, especially, has been reluctant to endorse staff facilities for fiscal analysis independent of its control. The committee would prefer to rely on its own professional staff (it has unlimited authority to hire such staff under the Reorganization Act) and upon special investigating teams drawn from the FBI, GAO, and other agencies.

A pre-audit budgetary function for the GAO would pose serious scheduling problems for House Appropriations. The Congress receives the budget in early January and the Appropriations staff begins reviewing the budget and agency justifications almost immediately. Unless the GAO is allowed to participate in the executive budget-formulation stage (a move some of its supporters advocate), the requirement of GAO review would further delay the appropriations process. Optional GAO participation in the appropriations process would depend on the willingness of House Appropriations to develop GAO as opposed to its own or other outside forms of staff assistance.

5. *Fear of a competitive legislative bureaucracy.* The separation of powers (separate legislative and executive roles) in the budget process has always contained the possibility of duplication of effort or open competition. Since establishing the Bureau of the Budget, Congress has been reluctant to create a parallel bureaucracy under the legislature, either through expanding the GAO or congressional staff. In the Senate debate prior to the passage of the McClellan bill, Senator Saltonstall and others warned against the possibility of a congressional Budget

---

[11] A further explanation for the Committee's disapproval is suggested by Robert Wallace, *op. cit.,* pp. 162-64. Lindsay Warren proposed "a modest beginning" with the government corporations—which were already subject to comprehensive commercial type audits under the Government Corporation Control Act. The Appropriations Committee recommended deferral "until a more complete and definite program can be evolved." Wallace feels that "the program was to be started where it was not necessary and where it would provide the least information."

Bureau, yet voted for passage.[12] Part of this congressional concern for safeguarding the executive role is also seen in the reluctance of Congress to push for the participation of GAO or appropriations staff in executive budget hearings. Robert Wallace has suggested that the Comptroller General, in a pre-audit role, could not avoid duplication in the appropriations process, but that he should steer clear of competition:

> GAO personnel should not formulate an independent budget, or hamstring administrative functions. They should stick with purely analytical and investigatory functions to provide Congress with data. If their information were not to conform with that furnished by the agencies, the latter should have ample opportunities to make their case.[13]

6. *Congressional reluctance to permit GAO entry into policy-making field.* While all five above

explanations have some validity, perhaps the most persuasive is one that escapes many of the advocates of reform via greater congressional reliance on the GAO.

Congress will not permit a bureaucratic staff unit to make effective political decisions on the budget. The pre- and post-audit functions differ importantly in the types of decisions required. In post-audit, the auditing agent essentially reviews the efficiency of program execution, given stated congressional policy and guidelines for administration. Pre-auditing is really budget analysis and review. While there is opportunity for important feedback from post-audit to budgetary review, the major decisions at the review stage are ones of allocation and funding levels. The GAO could review spending on highway programs but it is quite a different matter to allow it to decide whether funding should be at A, B, or C millions of dollars for a given fiscal year. Congress and its appointed

---

[12] *Congressional Record*, 82d Congress, 2d Session, April 7, 1952, pp. 3596-97. Various legislative proposals have since been introduced to set up a congressional budget office. The late Chairman Cannon of the House Appropriations Committee sponsored a bill to transfer the responsibility for preparation of the budget from the executive to the legislative branch. An Office of the United States Budget would be established in the legislative branch under the control and direction of the Commissioner General of the Budget, and directly responsible to the Congress. See House, Special Subcommittee of the Committee on Government Operations, *Hearings on H.R. 4009, H.R. 6558, and H.J. Res. 346: Congressional Control Over the Budget of the United States*, 84th Congress, 1st Session, 1955.

[13] *Op. cit.*, p. 165.

committees will make the policy decisions.[14] Accordingly, on major policy questions, no one will listen to the advice of a unit like the GAO that has no political "responsibility" for its actions. The possibilities for establishing a working relationship between the GAO and Congress similar to that between the Bureau of the Budget and the President is limited by the existence of the appropriations committees' staff and by the lack of a clear hierarchy in leadership.[15]

Summary. The GAO has been seen by members of the Congress since 1921 as one of the most promising avenues for reform of the congressional budgetary process. But even after the initial problem of adjustment to its new institutional roles, the GAO has been restricted by congressional attitudes toward economy in government and the fear of establishing a legislative bureaucracy. Two essentially structural problems have barred full congressional utilization of the GAO: the central position of the House Appropriations Committee with unlimited staffing authority and the question of who will provide political direction and control of the budgetary actions of the GAO. These problems would seem to preclude the GAO as a serious reform alternative, although the Congress might reach the point of frustration with the House Appropriations Committee where it would act over its head.[16] In any event, unless the Congress redefines the budgetary role of House Appropriations, the GAO would remain a permissive staff service. The concern of the reformer might better be focused on

[14] As one appropriations staff member noted, "Budget review is the responsibility of the congressman, not the General Accounting Office. Congress shouldn't evade its responsibility." Senator Moody expressed a similar view during the hearings on the Reorganization Act. "The question whether or not a function is necessary is a policy question. It is a function of Congress that cannot be decided by any commission." Senate, Committee on Expenditures in the Executive Departments, *Hearings: Organization and Operation of Congress,* 82d Congress, 1st Session, 1951, p. 185.

[15] The House Appropriations Committee has nonetheless used GAO reports extensively during its review of the budget. During the course of the 1964 appropriations hearings 86 GAO reports were reviewed and some 500 GAO findings used by the committee and subcommittees in their consideration and deliberations. See House, Subcommittee on Legislative Appropriations of the Committee on Appropriations, *Hearings: Legislative Branch Appropriations for 1965,* 88th Congress, 2d Session, 1964, p. 54.

[16] A reform proposal to "authorize the General Accounting Office to review all budget requests after they are submitted by the President, and increase the GAO's responsibility for reporting regularly to Congress on its audits of expenditures" received surprising support (75 percent in favor, 16 opposed, 10 undecided or no answer) in a recent survey of House members. See Roger H. Davidson, David Kovenock, and Michael O'Leary, *Congressional Reorganization: Problems and Prospects: Conference Working Papers* (Hanover, N.H.: Public Affairs Center, Dartmouth College, 1964), Appendices, p. 11.

the immediate question of Appropriations Committee staff.

Staffing the Appropriations Committee

Congressional efforts to staff the appropriations committees should be seen as part of a much broader movement to provide Congress with independent professional staff assistance. The Legislative Reorganization Act of 1946 marks the establishment of the congressional staff system—largely in reaction to the rapid development of executive research facilities to a near monopoly position under the Roosevelt Administration.[17] The staffing provisions of the Reorganization Act constitute, in effect, part of the congressional response to the differential development of executive and legislative roles since the Budgeting and Accounting Act of 1921. For reasons we have just noted Congress was reluctant to expand the role of the GAO. It was logical that it should turn its attention to staffing the key congressional elements in the system.

On the eve of the Reorganization Act, the House Appropriations Committee had eight clerks; the Senate committee, nine—supplemented by a few part-time investigators and accountants. Arthur Macmahon, writing in 1943, reflects the air of complacency surrounding "the focus of appropriations." The smallness of the staff, he observed, was offset by its continuity and experience (the House Committee had had only three chief clerks since its creation in 1865). The staff's "esprit de corps and cheerful procedural competence" served to discourage the movement for increased staffing.[18] The Joint Committee on the Organization of the Congress, however, took a decidedly more pessimistic view of Congress' "antiquated and inadequate appropriating machinery and practices." With hesitation, yet with a sense of duty, it urged that "the full committee and each subcommittee of the Appropriations Committees of the two Houses be given four expertly trained staff assistants."[19] Considering the preeminence of the appropriations process and the sums involved, the Joint Committee concluded that the Appropriations Committees should be "the best equipped of any committees of the Congress."

---

[17] For a discussion of congressional attitudes toward the predominance of executive staff see Ernest S. Griffith, *Congress: Its Contemporary Role* (3d ed.; New York: New York University Press, 1961), pp. 76-89.

[18] Macmahon, "Congressional Oversight of Administration—I," *loc. cit.*, p. 185.

[19] *Report: Organization of the Congress, op. cit.*, p. 21.

At the insistence of the leaders of the House Committee, including the new chairman, Clarence Cannon, this recommendation was replaced in the Legislative Reorganization Act by a provision authorizing the appropriations committees to employ whatever staff they considered necessary. Following the Reorganization Act the House committee increased its staff gradually to about 20 clerks—a level that has remained markedly stable since 1951.[20] Clerk stenographers and office help also have been increased from about 15 in 1947 to 30 to 40 since 1954. This latter group fluctuates with the budget season. (See Figure IV for a statistical summary of the staffs of the House and Senate Committees on Appropriations.) This permanent staff has never exceeded 60 and has averaged closer to 50 over the past two sessions.[21] The committee has chosen instead to develop its special investigating staff to handle increases in its work load. Two different approaches toward the use of the investigating staff have been evolved under Democratic (Clarence Cannon) and Republican (John Taber) control of the committee.

Under Mr. Cannon, the investigating staff functioned as an anonymous body with rotating membership which investigated problems on request and prepared reports for committee use. The Director of the Surveys and Investigation Staff was usually an FBI investigator retained by the committee for one or two years. Other members of the staff were taken from a variety of federal agencies on a short-term basis (from a few weeks to several months): FBI, GAO, Treasury, T.V.A., A.E.C., Civil Service Commission, Federal Power Commission, etc. Mr. Cannon explained the functioning of the investigating staff, as follows:

> The number of experts at the command of the Committee . . . is unlimited. . . . That is the advantage of our system. It is elastic. It can be ex-

---

[20] The variety of titles applied to committee staff and the intermixture of professional and clerical staff make classification difficult. See Kenneth Kofmehl, *Professional Staffs of Congress* (Purdue University Studies. Humanities Series; Purdue University Press, 1962), pp. 37-51. The staff of House Appropriations is here divided into regular and special investigatory. Regular staff are subdivided into clerks (upper level) and clerk stenographers (lower level assistants). The Senate Committee differentiates between clerks and professional staff members. See Figure IV.

[21] This figure includes about 10 clerk stenographers provided ranking minority members on the subcommittees, to relieve the burden appropriations work may place on regular office staff. These assistants are normally located in the members' offices and are not permitted to attend committee executive sessions.

panded or contracted. . . . We have a fresh group on every inquiry. And new brooms sweep clean. . . . I do not see a single man who makes these investigations. We have an FBI man in charge, and when an investigation is to be made, the requisition, signed by the ranking majority and minority members of the subcommittee and the committee, is transmitted by the clerk to the FBI man and the FBI man selects the operators who he considers are qualified. The chairman never comes in contact with him or any of the agents; and the minority have as much access to the information they supply as the majority.[22]

In summary, an effort was made to keep staff investigations as nonpartisan and objective as possible by screening committee members from investigators.

The approach used under Mr. Taber differed in two regards. A special effort was made to recruit professional personnel from outside the government as consultants on contract to the committee for $50 a day. Some of the best talent in industry, finance, and private professional organizations was tapped— U.S. Steel, the National City Bank of New York, the National Association of State Chambers of Commerce, and the American Institute of Accountants. These consultants soon won the nicknames "dollar detectives" and "copper cops." (Two of them later became directors of the Bureau of the Budget.) The consultants worked with a small permanent professional staff drawn from the FBI, GAO, and Treasury. A second important difference was the close association of the investigating staff with members of the committee. The staff maintained contact with the relevant subcommittees, prepared summaries and digests of their reports, and even gave briefings at meetings of the subcommittees. The Taber staff gained a reputation for "stirring things up" that has been applauded by some members, and criticized by others, for being "too political." It generated some friction with the regular permanent staff of the committee. Since the Democrats regained control of Congress the Cannon system has been reinstituted.[23]

[22] *Congressional Record*, 82d Congress, 1st Session, March 22, 1951, pp. 2803-05.

[23] One member interviewed suggested that the regular committee staff, on the basis of this experience, has since preferred the strict screening process and isolation of investigatory staff from the members. Under the new chairman, George H. Mahon, there may be more flexibility in the use of the investigating staff, according to the preference of the individual subcommittee chairmen.

The regular staff of Senate Appropriations has undergone a similar increase since the Reorganization Act. Its current strength has stabilized at about 30—8 clerks, 14 "professional" staff, and 8 clerical assistants (see Figure IV).[24] However, it has not developed an investigating staff comparable to the House Committee. The committee did gain a small foreign aid investigating staff in the early fifties which was transferred in 1955 to the McClellan Permanent Investigations Subcommittee of the Senate Committee on Government Operations.

The leaderships of the two appropriations committees appear generally satisfied with the quality and amount of staff assistance. However, lower ranking members of the committees, and the membership of Congress at large favor increased staffing.[25] The House Appropriations Committee, the primary focus of the appropriations process, is most frequently criticized. Its 50 members, as we have noted, are serviced *directly* by some 20 upper level staff and a total staff of about 50, indirectly by a varying number of special investigators. The committee has resisted pressures to vary this pattern. It has also thwarted efforts to develop staff assistance independent of the committee. The maneuvering on the McClellan-Colmer bills in 1952 which would have established a Joint Budget Committee with professional staff provides a good illustration.

The McClellan bill (S. 913, 82d Congress) had been passed by the Senate on April 8, 1952 by a vote of 55-8. A companion bill—the Colmer bill (H.R. 7888) was reported from the Rules Committee on June 20. Before the rule providing for consideration of the Colmer bill came before the House,

[24] The Senate Appropriations Committee makes a distinction between clerks and professional staff members. George Galloway notes that "no administrative analysts or professional staff have been employed by the House committee 'because of a conviction that professional and clerical staff impede each other'. . . . During the Eightieth Congress, on the other hand, the Senate Appropriations Committee took advantage of the [Reorganization] act's authority to recruit a professional staff of eight experienced persons in addition to the regular clerical and investigative force." "Operation of Legislative Reorganization Act of 1946," *loc. cit.,* p. 640.

[25] See the debate between Chairman Cannon and Congressman Colmer, *Congressional Record,* 82d Congress, 1st Session, March 21, 1951, pp. 2803-05. Mr. Colmer argued that Appropriations did not have enough staff "to compete and to fight with . . . the experts that the departments have." This view was repeated by several members of the Committee interviewed by the author. One felt that the Defense subcommittee required 18 or 20 staff members to examine subjects in its jurisdiction—defense procurement, research and development, etc. Another suggested an overall staff in the vicinity of 500 would be adequate and that the junior members on the committee, with 10 years or less service, "all agree on this."

Chairman Cannon made an un-precedented move. The House had completed action on all appropriations bills by this stage of the session (July 2) but the Senate committee was working late into the night to complete action on the supplemental appropriations bill. At 11:20 p.m. on July 2d, a letter from Chairman Cannon requesting a new item of $500,000 for additional staff for House Appropriations was received by the Senate Appropriations Committee. The request was included as an amendment to the bill in keeping with the general understanding or "rule of comity" that each house should be free to determine matters internal to itself. Senator McClellan, who had been out of the committee room at the time and who did not discover the maneuver until the following day, was quick to see the effect, but too late. Although he did succeed in adding the Joint Budget Committee as an amendment to the bill, the House supporters of the Colmer bill, temporarily disarmed, lost the roll call vote on the rule, 155 to 173—one of those rare instances when the House has defeated a rule approved by its Rules Committee.[26] The con-ference committee struck the proposal for the Joint Budget Committee but earmarked $250,000 annually for each committee for additional staff.

Why has the House Committee on Appropriations resisted pressure to enlarge its staff at this critical focus in the congressional budget process? Why has it not provided itself with a more adequate permanent professional staff? This immediately raises the question, "adequate for what purposes?"—a question we shall defer until the next section. We can note at this point, however, some of the arguments against increased committee staffing in general that have collectively served to discourage efforts to enlarge committee staff.

1. *Increased staff may increase competition between the executive and legislative branches.* This is a common argument against congressional self-assertion in the budgetary process as noted in the case of the GAO. The fear is expressed that enlarged Appropriations staff (and especially a joint appropriations staff) might begin to usurp executive roles or needlessly duplicate them.[27] This fear appears to be

---

[26] See esp. speeches by Senator McClellan and Congressman Colmer, *Congressional Record,* 82d Congress, 2d Session, July 3, 1952, pp. 9141, 9224-27.

[27] Arthur Macmahon's conclusion is typical: "Staffing might easily be pushed to a point where it would bring a legislative budget method into existence in rivalry with the executive budget. An ambiguous responsibility might develop in the departments. There is need for the most careful consideration, not glib endorsement of the idea

overrated. Congress is unlikely to assume the major responsibilities of executive budget formulation. In any event, it is the American separation of powers that introduces tension between executive and legislative roles, not the existence of staff. We should look instead at the potential of staff in developing the budgetary roles of the various participants.

2. *Increased staff poses problems for congressional control. Committee staff may develop into independent power centers.* Some members of Congress, not the least the late Clarence Cannon, have voiced concern that large permanent committee staffs will get out of congressional control:

> What happens when you put men permanently on the staff? They get careless. They get lazy. They develop friendships with the departments. If you get misfits it is hard to fire

them. They develop a camaraderie with the members of the committee and get their salaries raised. . . . When there is no investigation they sit around cooling their heels and their time and their salary is wasted.[28]

Staff members may become "wheelers and dealers." Several members and staff personnel interviewed questioned the wisdom of granting too much power to the staff. The experience of the Joint Committee on Atomic Energy was cited in this regard. Two reservations to this argument should be noted. First it assumes an essentially negative view of bureaucracy that does not fit the experience of most committees since the Reorganization Act. Secondly it underestimates the ability of congressmen individually and collectively to keep order in their own house.

3. *By increasing staff to gain*

of staff and more staff." "Congressional Oversight of Administration: I," *loc. cit.,* p. 187. ·Ralph Huitt, *loc. cit.,* pp. 436-39, raises this and other criticisms of proposals to increase committee staff, concluding that "the committee's judgment is entitled to a good deal of respect."

[28] *Congressional Record,* 82nd Congress, 1st Session, March 21, 1951, p. 2804. The goal of isolating staff from executive agency counterparts may be both unrealistic and undesirable. Bertram Gross observes that members of Congress "need the expertise that can be obtained only from people who have been intimately engaged in the operations of executive agencies and private organizations. In many instances skilled congressional staff members are needed primarily to serve as organizers of staff work outside Congress, or as intermediaries through whom staff experts outside Congress can present their work to the members and committees of Congress." *The Legislative Struggle: A Study in Social Combat* (McGraw-Hill Series in Political Science; New York: McGraw-Hill, 1953), p. 421. Both Macmahon and Gross suggest a positive role for staff in effecting improved executive-legislative relations.

greater expertise congressmen run the risk of sacrificing the lay element in legislative thinking—their unique contribution. Arthur Macmahon argues that congressmen, immediately in touch with their constituents, have a duty to bring "practical public sense" to bear in the oversight of administration. They also introduce their criticism of a "robust imaginative lay mind" into technical operations. These values might be lost if the politician-legislator dealt with administration vicariously through an intermediate legislative bureaucracy.[29] Again, this line of argument, which is widely held by political scientists, needs qualification. The introduction of staff does not preclude direct legislator-administrator dealings—it may even increase them by giving the legislator more to talk about. As the complexity of public policy issues increases, more staff assistance will be required to maintain intelligent or informed dialogue. So long as the legislator is subject to reelection and the administrator is responsible for implementing a program there is little likelihood that the mingling of non-special and special minds will be lost.

Members of the House frequently cite the dependence of senators on comparatively large staffs—both committee and office—as an argument against increased House staffing. Again, staffing is not the cause but more nearly an effect—an effect of the number of committee and subcommittee assignments held by each senator and of the size of the constituency he represents.

4. *Increased staffing will make no difference in the outcome of appropriations decisions.* Under this view committee staffs already provide "more bullets, grist, possibilities for cuts" than the committee can take. As one staff member put it, "only so much can go through the small end of the funnel." Political will, not information, is the limiting factor to further economies. Staff personnel could be trebled or quadrupled and it would not effect the end result. As Senator Dworshak observed during the 1951 hearings on the Reorganization Act of 1946:

> The staffs are adequate and do a splendid job. The members of the staff, however, cannot force the members of the Appropriations Committee to make a cut of 1 percent, 5 percent, 10 percent or 20 percent. The only way to cut is to cut. The members of the Senate and the House frequently are reluctant to make a reduction in appropriations. . . . Then

---

[29] Macmahon, "Oversight of Administration: I," *loc. cit.,* p. 187.

we have no economy and no reduction in the cost of operating the Federal Government. Congress cannot pass the buck to committees and staff.[30]

This view assumes that economy or budget cutting per se is the test of the effectiveness of the appropriations process. Senator Moody's reply to Senator Dworshak points out a major shortcoming of the argument, however:

> In my judgment, whenever a committee . . . comes up with a blanket cut, that is a confession that they have not been able to find ways for the money to be saved. Either they do not want to cut the individual items and do not have the gumption to do so, or they cannot find or do not know where the money should be saved . . . that shows a lack of adequate grounding in the details of the budget. Therefore it seems to me that the Appropriations Committee needs more staff.[31]

While congressional budgetary decisions represent political judgments, professional staffs can assist Congress by providing greater rationality to such decisions.

5. *Increased staffing is an unjustified form of extravagance for a committee concerned with economy.* This attitude, noted also in regard to the GAO, derives support from several of the previous arguments. It also assumes a negative view of staff bureaucracy and sees few additional economies resulting from an increase in staff personnel.

* * * * * *

This cluster of attitudes suggests some of the reasons why the appropriations staff has resisted enlargement (and why some of the advocates of budgetary reform outside the Congress have opposed this approach).[32] But it is only a partial explanation. Several structural and situational factors have permitted these attitudes, which one might fairly describe as "parochial," to survive.

The seniority system provides a kind of "built-in stabilizer." For congressional committee members, access to staff assistance diminishes in inverse relationship to seniority and position—from the chairman and ranking minority member, to

---

[30] *Hearings: Organization and Operation of Congress, op. cit.,* p. 187.

[31] *Ibid.*

[32] An additional argument against staff assumes that close congressional attention to detail is undesirable and that increases in staff will reinforce procedures that are themselves inadequate. See Smithies, *op. cit.,* pp. 163, 167-74.

subcommittee chairmen and ranking minority members, down. The individuals in the position to do most about staffing the committee have a virtual monopoly of the staff—and are much less apt to see a need for increased staff. Junior members—who may include a sizable number of "activists" or "legislative technicians"—feel the need for staff assistance more acutely but lack the power to obtain it.[33]

To an extent, the staffing of the appropriations committees is a problem of the generations. The older generation — including the leaderships of these committees—has served in Congress through the period of major budgetary expansion. Techniques of budgetary control and patterns of staff assistance that served them two decades or longer ago have been adapted to the present situation. This tight staffing control provides both a sense of continuity or security in approach and a means for staying on top of the younger members who would like to develop new uses for staff in reviewing the budget.

Finally, we should note that the limited view of staffing held by some of the senior members of the House Appropriations Committee is consistent with the tendency of the committee to keep information to itself. A good part of the demand for increased staff comes from rank and file members who feel the need for professional staff assistance in understanding the budget and the recommendations of the Appropriations Committee—staff assistance not now readily available from either the Budget Bureau or the Committee staff. This is quite a different use of staff over and above what the appropriations member might consider adequate.

Summary. Congress acted in 1946 to provide itself and especially its appropriations committees' with professional staff to counter the growth of executive staff resources. This move has been frustrated, however, by the House Appropriations Committee which has resisted pressures to increase its staff. Several arguments against increased staffing have been expressed within and without the Congress—especially the dangers of a competitive, independent staff bureaucracy, usurping both executive roles and congressional powers. These arguments tend to overstate the risks and

[33] One senior staff member of House Appropriations interviewed was not aware that any members of the committee were dissatisfied with the staffing arrangements. This may be explained by the fact that the staff spend most of their time working for ranking members and have less direct association with younger members. Also younger members serve an "apprentice" role and are expected to keep quiet. See Fenno, *loc. cit.*, pp. 318-19.

ignore possible gains or wider objectives that might be served by staff enlargement. Staffing reform is also impeded by the seniority system and the tendency to restrict the information-service functions of appropriations staff primarily to members of the committee. To the extent that attitudes toward staffing divide along lines of the older and newer generations of members, one would expect a broader conception of staffing to emerge when leadership passes to the newer generation.[34]

Congressional Attempts to Establish a Legislative Budget

The Legislative Reorganization Act of 1946, in addition to providing the Congress with professional committee staff, attempted to meet some of the major criticisms of the congressional budget process directly. The Report of the Joint Committee on the Organization of the Congress, noting the divided authority that existed between the Houses, between the control of revenues and expenditures, and within the respective appropriations committees, asked "how could Congress have a general fiscal policy or follow it if it had one?"[35] The solution reached in section 138 of the final legislation was a "legislative budget." The four major fiscal committees (House Ways and Means, House Appropriations, Senate Finance, and Senate Appropriations) were to meet jointly at the beginning of each regular session to consider the budget recommendations of the President and to report a legislative budget to their respective Houses by February 15 (the Joint Committee had recommended April 15). The legislative budget was to include estimated overall federal receipts and expenditures for the ensuing fiscal year, and to be accompanied by a concurrent resolution fixing a ceiling to total appropriations. Budget surpluses would be applied to reduction of the debt and budget deficits would require explicit prior congressional approval. In the latter case the concurrent resolution would include a section stating "that it is the sense of the Congress that the public debt

---

[34] The accession of George Mahon to the chairmanship of House Appropriations may signal some changes in the attitudes of the committee leadership toward staffing although it is too early to determine what they will be. Mahon's subcommittee, Defense Appropriations, has had the largest staff of any of the appropriations subcommittees.

[35] *Report: Organization of the Congress, op. cit.,* p. 18. The Joint Committee went on to recommend a much more drastic solution than was incorporated in the final version of the act. Mandatory cuts by a uniform percentage were provided in the event that total appropriations exceeded the total budget limit set by Congress. *Ibid.,* pp. 18-19.

shall be increased in an amount equal to the amount by which the estimated expenditures for the ensuing fiscal year exceed the estimated receipts, such amount being $——.''

The legislative budget and the Joint Committee set up to effect it were seen as major steps toward strengthening congressional control of the purse, by rationalizing the congressional budget process and providing Congress with the mechanism to debate and determine broad fiscal policy. As Senator Monroney later observed, "the idea behind the legislative budget was for high-level debate on just how much the government could afford to spend and how much we could raise in taxes, and then try to fix a target beyond which total appropriations should not go."[36]

Three attempts to implement the legislative budget failed. In 1947 both Houses passed concurrent resolutions but the conference deadlocked on how to divide the anticipated surplus between tax reduction and debt retirement. In 1948 a ceiling was set but subsequently disregarded by the appropriations committees and Congress which passed appropriations exceeding the legislative budget by some $6 billion. In 1949 the legislative budget was postponed, by concurrent resolution, to May 1, but by that time 11 appropriations bills had passed in the House, nine in the Senate. No budget was reported that year or since and section 138 has become a dead letter provision. Of the major provisions of the Act, the legislative budget has been considered the least successful by senators and House members.[37] George Galloway concludes that while the aim of the legislative budget is generally regarded as "laudable" in congressional circles, "experience with it seems to have shown that the instrument is not properly suited to its task."[38]

Why did the legislative budget fail? Was it due to errors in method and technique or errors in basic conception? Partially both, it appears. The experience with the legislative budget suggests some of the pitfalls that broad or general reforms can encounter when they are drafted hastily without adequate reference to the functioning or the power structure of the given system.

1. *The Joint Committee on the Legislative Budget was not constituted or staffed on a realistic basis.*

[36] *Hearings: Organization and Operation of Congress, op. cit.,* p. 159.

[37] *Ibid.,* pp. 7-8. "Questionnaire on Congressional Reorganization submitted to 67 Senators, 263 Members of the House of Representatives," December 1950.

[38] *Ibid.,* p. 639, "Operation of Legislative Reorganization Act of 1946."

A Joint Committee of 102 members was obviously unwieldy and was reduced to a subcommittee of about 20 members which did the detailed work on the legislative budget. But, as Senator Styles Bridges explained: "We had no staff; we had no assistants. The whole budget proposition was thrown at us, and it had to be worked out within a limited time. If a legislative budget set-up is to be successful, I think you have to have a continuing committee. It has to be small, and it has to be adequately staffed."[39]

Senator Monroney made the following post mortem: "It never became a fixed part of our operations. It became more or less a political symbol. We are going to cut $6 billion, we said, and everybody is in favor of cutting it $6 billion without knowing how to do it."[40]

Why did the Congress neglect to set up and staff an adequate Joint Committee? Part of the answer lies in the attitudes toward staffing noted above, i.e., that budget cutting requires political will, not staffing. It may also be that Congress had no real appreciation of the work involved in a legislative budget when it took it on. And there exists the very real possibility that important elements within Congress did not want the experiment to succeed.[41] The later open opposition of the House Committee on Appropriations to the McClellan Joint Budget Committee with a separate joint staff is suggestive. And supporters of the President's program within Congress might have feared that greater congressional control of the budget would mean a more effective economy drive (especially where a Democratic President faced a Republican Congress after the 1946 elections).[42]

2. *The scheduling of the legislative budget did not leave adequate time for Joint Committee consid-*

---

[39] *Ibid.,* p. 522.

[40] *Ibid.,* p. 160.

[41] Holbert Carroll concludes that "the experiment actually never had a fair trial. A majority of the members of the appropriations committees of the House and Senate were lukewarm about the experiment and never gave it adequate support. The party leaders of the House, especially the Democratic leaders, did not like the idea of a legislative budget." *Op. cit.,* p. 198.

[42] Aaron Wildavsky sees this as a logical implication of the Joint Committee mechanism. ". . . the membership of the Joint Committee would be made up largely of conservatives from safe districts who are not dependent on the President, who come from a different constituency than he does, but with whom he must deal in order to get any money for his programs. Should the Joint Committee ever be able to command a two-thirds vote of the Congress, it could virtually ignore the President in matters of domestic policy and run the executive branch so that it is accountable only to them." "Political Implications of Budgetary Reform," *loc cit.,* p. 186.

eration. At the same time it delayed the normal legislative work of the respective fiscal committees. Even if the Joint Committee had been adequately staffed, it could not have completed work on the legislative budget by February 15. Consideration of the budget might be advanced prior to official presidential submission but this probably would be resisted by the executive.[43] The appropriations subcommittees would oppose pushing the date back. When this was done in 1949, the appropriations subcommittees proceeded with their hearings independently and any semblance of Joint Committee influence on the appropriations process disappeared.

3. *Congress was reluctant to commit itself to a legislative budget prior to detailed consideration of the separate appropriations requests.*[44] When it did vote a ceiling, it became a political symbol with no binding effect on the appropriations committees. The actual determination of appropriations continued to be from the base up. Congress apparently still believed that a minute appraisal of expenditure requests by the appropriate appropriations subcommittee was required before

final action could be taken. As Clarence Cannon observed, "we can no more expect success . . . with this well-meant but hopeless proposal than we can expect a verdict from the jury before it has heard the evidence."[45]

The attempt to impose budgetary decisions on the system broke down because there was no adequate hierarchical power structure to enforce them. Aaron Wildavsky has concluded that no effective joint committee *determination* of the budget is possible in the American system because "there is no cohesive group in Congress capable of using these devices to affect decision making by imposing its preferences on a majority of congressmen.[46] It is not surprising that the Wherry resolution of 1949 to streamline the Joint Committee included no provision for adoption of the budget by concurrent resolution.

*   *   *   *   *

What can we conclude from the experience of the Joint Committee on the legislative budget? One conclusion that has been drawn is that Congress should leave budget making to the executive branch, which

---

[43] See testimony of Senator Francis Case, *Hearings: Organization and Operation of Congress, op. cit.,* pp. 342-43.

[44] See *Financial Management in the Federal Government, op. cit.,* pp. 29-31.

[45] *Congressional Record,* 81st Congress, 1st Session, February 7, 1949, pp, 879-82.

[46] Wildavsky, "Political Implications of Budgetary Reform," *loc cit.,* p. 186.

is better equipped for the task. Instead Congress should "review" the President's budget, using the budget document as a frame of reference to coordinate its several committees. Robert Wallace concludes that review is a "proper role," since the purpose of Congress is "to harmonize the interests of hundreds of different constituencies, rather than to propose overall fiscal policy."[47]

Yet the sentiment in Congress for a Joint Committee on Fiscal Policy remains high in spite of the disappointing experience with the legislative budget. A recent survey of congressional attitudes toward congressional reorganization completed by the Dartmouth Public Affairs Center indicated 62 percent in favor, 28 percent opposed, and 10 percent undecided or not answering on the proposal for such a Joint Committee.[48] If Congress is to be in a position to review fiscal policy or to initiate action in those instances when the executive does not provide leadership, some type of a joint committee mechanism would appear to be essential.

The lessons of 1947-49 are that such a committee, if it is to succeed, should be streamlined and adequately staffed, and should operate on a continuous basis. Rigid pre-announced budget ceilings should be replaced by a more flexible system that better accords with the structure of committee power. Congress has not yet exhausted the possibilities of this approach to budgetary reform.

The Omnibus Appropriations Bill

Shortly after the demise of the legislative budget, Congress attempted another innovation to enhance its control of spending—the omnibus or consolidated appropriations bill. The idea was first pressed by Senator Harry Byrd, although it was at Chairman Clarence Cannon's initiative that the dozen separate appropriations bills were tied into a single package during the consideration of the fiscal year 1951 budget in 1950. The omnibus appropriations approach had similar objectives to those of the legislative budget, but on a reduced scale. Both provided Congress with an overview of spending that it had not theretofore had. Both focused on the expenditure as opposed to the revenue side of the equation. Both were seen as means for achieving

---

[47] Wallace, *op. cit.,* pp. 152-53. Huitt also concludes "the role of Congress is not to shape a unified policy but to respond to one." *Loc cit.,* p. 408.

[48] Davidson, Kovenock, and O'Leary, *op. cit.,* appendices, p. 8. The specific proposal was to "create a 'Joint Committee on Fiscal Policy' composed of members of House and Senate appropriations and revenue committees to give broad consideration and direction to federal spending."

greater economies during congressional review of the executive budget. However, they differed in one crucial regard. In the legislative budget procedure, the Joint Committee had set the guidelines; under the consolidated appropriations approach, the House Appropriations Committee would draw up the omnibus bill and in effect set the agenda for congressional debate. When combined with the staffing practices of the committee, the omnibus bill gave House Appropriations a significant increase in leverage within the House—an effect we shall examine presently. Against Mr. Cannon's wishes, the experiment was abandoned after one year, due to strong opposition from the Senate, the rank and file membership of the House, and a majority of his own committee. The idea still has support from the exponents of a more rational budget process, although usually qualified by the addition of an item veto.[49] George Galloway has described it

as "a forward step in appropriations procedure" giving the country a picture of the total outlay contemplated for the fiscal year and allowing Congress to see "the claims of spending pressure groups in relation to the total national fiscal picture."[50] Arthur Smithies concludes that, with simplified program-budgeting procedures which would enable Congress to consider broad policy rather than detail, the omnibus bill "has much to commend it."[51] Why then does the omnibus bill enjoy such little support within Congress? In the same survey that found 62 percent of the House members polled favoring a Joint Committee on Fiscal Policy, the single omnibus appropriations bill was supported by only 14 percent, opposed by 82 percent, with the balance expressing no opinion.[52] Several factors have contributed to the unpopularity of the omnibus approach.

1. *The consolidated appropriations bill aroused the opposition of*

---

[49] See "The Federal Budget—There Must Be a Better Way," *The Morgan Guaranty Survey* (New York: Morgan Guaranty Trust Company, April 1964), pp. 3-12.

[50] "Operation of Legislative Reorganization Act of 1946," *loc. cit.*, p. 641. See also "Reform of the Federal Budget," *Public Affairs Bulletin No. 80* (Washington: Legislative Reference Service, Library of Congress, 1950), pp. 96-97, for a discussion of the arguments for the omnibus approach. For another favorable assessment of the omnibus approach see Dalmas H. Nelson, "The Omnibus Act of 1950," *Journal of Politics*, May 1953, pp. 275-88.

[51] Smithies, *op. cit.*, pp. 99-100. Holbert Carroll also concludes that an omnibus bill "permits a more rational coordination of foreign policy appropriations with other appropriations intimately associated with foreign affairs such as for national defense." *Op. cit.*, p. 205.

[52] Of 32 reform suggestions, the omnibus appropriations bill ranked 31st.

numerous interest groups whose range of maneuver was limited by the reform. This was the major cause for congressional hostility, in Mr. Cannon's view. "Much of the antagonism to the consolidated bill has come from outside the committee. Every predatory lobbyist, every pressure group seeking to get its hands into the . . . Treasury, every bureaucrat seeking to extend his empire" had opposed it, not to mention members of Congress who were "beneficiaries of Federal largess distributed in their districts and their States."[53] The chairman's success in cutting the rivers and harbors "pork barrel" appropriations by one-fourth via the omnibus approach was bound to produce some reaction. Yet the resistance to the omnibus bill was not simply the spenders vs. the economizers, as Mr. Cannon suggested.

2. *The omnibus approach disrupted established congressional work procedures,* causing delays and placing strains on other parts of the system. Under the omnibus approach a central subcommittee was set up within House Appropriations to coordinate the work of the separate subcommittees.[54] What had previously been a dozen separate bills were reviewed by the new sub-

committee and held in committee until they could be reported simultaneously—as chapters of a 427-page bill. (The bill actually was reported without the foreign aid chapter, which had not yet received its annual authorization.)   For six weeks in March and April the Appropriations Committee led the debate on the bill on the House floor —an unusual length of time for a single committee to command the attention of the House. The Senate committee could not begin hearing agency appeals until the entire bill had passed the House. Noncontroversial appropriations bills that usually passed early in the session were delayed. It is not surprising that the subcommittee chairmen of Senate Appropriations were unanimous in their opposition to the omnibus idea. Members of legislative committees also complained that their bills were being delayed. Supporters of the reform claimed that it expedited consideration of appropriations bills and that it had the net effect of reducing the amount of time required for the congressional appropriations process. Most observers, however, feel that it introduced important delays into the system.[55]

3. *The omnibus bill weakened*

[53] *Congressional Record*, 82d Congress, 1st Session, January 29, 1951, p. 768.

[54] *Ibid.*, pp. 764-68.

[55] Wallace, *op. cit.*, pp. 134-35.

the position of the individual congressman versus the Appropriations Committee in the congressional budget process. As we have noted, there has been an historic tension between the Appropriations Committee and the House—a fear of too much power being concentrated in a single committee of the Congress. We have also noted the tendency of the House Appropriations Committee to resolve differences within the committee and to present an integrated, nonpartisan front to the House. The practice of separate appropriations bills has afforded interested members the time to study the work of the committee, to debate recommendations on the floor, and to mobilize support for individual amendments.[56] The omnibus bill, however, served to integrate the Appropriations Committee too much. While affording an opportunity for general debate on broad policy alternatives, it eliminated much of the traditional means for checking the committee.[57] It implied a new relationship

between member and committee that the House membership was not ready to accept. Robert Wallace has observed:

> The main value of committee study is to save time for individual Members of Congress and permit them to devote themselves to items for which they feel the committee did not recommend proper amounts. The value of the committee is lost if there is not sufficient time to review its recommendations and to study particular items before the general floor debate takes place.[58]

The concern of the individual member can be dismissed as merely seeking benefits for local interests (Mr. Cannon's explanation). Even if it were limited to this, one can see partial justification — as long as one admits that some degree of local representation is desirable in the congressional budget process. But the member's concern goes deeper than this. The fact that he

---

[56] See Congressman Clem Miller's discussion of the difficulty of tackling the Appropriations Committee on the floor of the House. Baker, ed., *op. cit.*, pp. 39-41.

[57] Chairman Cannon argued that the procedure made more information available to the members and press earlier. ". . . transcripts were published periodically by installments, as hearings progressed, instead of being held until the bill was finished and the hearings finally published in one ponderous volume as heretofore. . . . releases were made to the press and to the public periodically from the beginning of the hearings to the close." *Congressional Record*, 82d Congress, 1st Session, January 25, 1951, p. 767. However, the *decisions* of the subcommittees were held until the consolidated bill was reported. This was the real focus of criticism.

[58] Wallace, *op. cit.*, p. 135

must vote on appropriations — all appropriations— casts him in a *national* role as well. He may simply take his signals from the committee, members on it whose judgment he trusts, or from his party leadership. On the other hand he may want to examine an issue himself and make his own determination. In both cases the committee is in theory the member's agent. In the case of the omnibus appropriations bill, members may well have felt overwhelmed by the avalanche of items for consideration that descended on them at one time.

4. *The omnibus bill is open more to horizontal than to selective reductions, and is particularly vulnerable to legislative riders.*[59] While selective reductions may be accomplished within committee, once the bill reaches the floor the pressure may grow for across-the-board reductions or meat-axe cuts. In the 1950 case, the House voted on the last day of debate to cut some $600 million in an across-the-board percentage reduction in personnel and administrative services. In the Senate a rider was added to the bill (the Bridges-Byrd amendment) requiring a further reduction of $550 million to be apportioned at the discretion of the President. Ironically, the very effort to introduce greater

rationality into the appropriations process—by providing an overview of appropriations—has produced other irrationalities. Senator Mc-Clellan put his finger on the problem in the 1951 hearings on the Reorganization Act:

> That is our need, to be able to make intelligent cuts. . . . We have not had the information which would enable us to do that. We have resorted to the device of the over-all blanket cut which is not sound. We do that in desperation.[60]

Summary. The omnibus appropriations bill might have succeeded where the legislative budget failed. It was integrated into the committee structure of the House Appropriations Committee instead of being a potential competitor to it. Yet this, by strengthening the position of House Appropriations within the system, contributed as much to its rejection as any other cause. Again the tendency toward horizontal reductions suggests that the same staff informational deficiencies that undermined the legislative budget were also present in the omnibus appropriations bill. After the experience of 1950 the Congress seems inclined to try approaches other than the omnibus bill in its efforts

---

[59] Carroll, *op. cit.*, p. 206.

[60] *Hearings: Organization and Operation of Congress, op. cit.*, p. 191.

to strengthen congressional control of federal spending.

The Joint Committee on the Budget

Of the various reform proposals advanced since 1950, the McClellan bill to establish a Joint Committee on the Budget has had the most serious congressional support.[61] Not to be confused with the defunct Joint Committee on the Legislative Budget, the Joint Committee on the Budget which would have 14 members, divided evenly between the House and Senate Appropriations Committees (hence the alternate description, Joint Appropriations Committee). Offered as a substitute amendment to section 138 of the Legislative Reorganization Act, it has won the endorsement of some of the original supporters of section 138[62] and has undergone successive refinements over the 14 years since Senator McClellan introduced it in February 1950. It was passed by the Senate in 1952, 1953, 1955, 1957, 1961, and 1963—the last five occasions without recorded dissent. The House Appropriations Committee has blocked its adoption

in the House since the near success of the Colmer bill in 1952.[63] Over this period the advocates and opponents of the Joint Budget Committee have had ample time to develop their cases.

In its current form the McClellan bill[64] would establish a 14-member "joint service committee" with seven members each from House and Senate Appropriations—divided on a four to three majority-minority party ratio.[65] The chairmanship would rotate between the Houses on alternate years, with the other body holding the vice-chairmanship. The committee would have a staff director appointed by and responsible to the party of the chairman, and an associate staff director appointed by and responsible to the members of the opposition party—an explicit recognition of party roles in the congressional budget process. It would be authorized to hire "such other professional, technical, clerical, and other employees, temporary or permanent," without regard to civil service laws

---

[61] For a legislative history of the bill see *Financial Management in the Federal Government, op. cit.,* pp. 195-216.

[62] See for example the testimony of Carter W. Atkins, Executive Director, Connecticut Public Expenditure Council, *Hearings: Organization and Operation of Congress, op. cit.,* p. 230. The Council has been credited for the original concept of a Joint Committee on the Budget in the 1946 Act.

[63] *Supra,* pp. 48-49.

[64] S.537, 88th Congress, 1st Session.

[65] The Colmer bill provided for a nine to seven House-Senate membership ratio.

or limitations on compensation, as would be necessary to carry out the duties of the committee. The Comptroller General would be given the authority to undertake, at the request of the chairman, budgetary pre-audit investigations and reports. Professional and technical employees of the Joint Committee would have broad investigative authority, including access to "the fiscal books, documents, papers, and reports of any Federal agency."

The duties of the Joint Committee would be: (1) to inform itself on all matters relating to the annual budget of the agencies of the U.S. Government, (2) to provide the respective appropriations committees information to enable "adequate consideration" of items contained in the budget and justifications submitted in their support, (3) to consider the President's messages on the State of the Union and the Economic Report, revenue estimates, and changing economic conditions, (4) to report its findings on budget estimates and revisions in appropriations to the respective Appropriations Committees, (5) to make reports and recommendations to the legislative committees that would effect greater efficiency and economy in government and cooperation between the authorizing and appropriating committees, and (6) to

compile cost estimates of all programs and projects authorized by Congress. The bill also would authorize the Joint Committee to recommend joint appropriations hearings and to loan staff to the appropriations committees. Staff members of the Bureau of the Budget would be assigned to attend executive sessions of the appropriations subcommittees at the request of the Committee or any of its subcommittees. Other provisions of the bill require the President's budget to contain special analyses on long-term construction and development programs, agency reports on the utilization of borrowing authority, and the submission on request of the Joint Committee of agency appropriation estimates on an annual accrued expenditure basis.

In summary, the McClellan bill proposes to develop various reforms Congress has previously rejected or failed to implement. It also proposes to close other loopholes that have limited the effectiveness of congressional control. The arguments advanced in support of the Joint Committee on the Budget are essentially four.[66] First, the Joint Committee would afford Congress the opportunity for coordinated study of the entire budget and continuing review of the nation's budgetary situation, i.e., it would introduce

---

[66] Condensed from my testimony, *Hearings on S.537*, pp. 51-53.

greater rationality into congressional procedures for considering the budget. Second, the Joint Committee approach develops two additional alternative sources of staff assistance. It creates a joint appropriations staff on the model of the Joint Committee on Internal Revenue Taxation and it enlists the GAO in a supporting budget review role. These, as we have noted, are not new ideas, but they have been given new expression in the McClellan proposal. Third, the Joint Committee should facilitate closer cooperation and working relationships between the two appropriations committees. Joint staff would not only increase the efficiency and speed of the appropriations process, avoiding unnecessary duplication of staff work, but would also provide precedents in the development of techniques of cooperation. Fourth, numerous provisions of the bill would serve to close loopholes in congressional control afforded by the dual structure of authorization versus appropriation committees. The Joint Committee would compile data on the total picture of authorizations and appropriations not currently available to Congress. By means of reports and recommendations to the legislative committees, the Joint Committee could facilitate a closer articulation between the two processes.

In view of these potential benefits, why has Congress—in this case the House—been so reluctant to implement the McClellan bill? Several answers have already been suggested. Drawing as it does on three of the approaches already considered by the Congress—the use of a joint committee mechanism, the increase of appropriations staff, and the development of a role for the GAO in budget review—the McClellan bill has drawn together a range of opposition. This opposition stems from the House Appropriations Committee, jealous of its prerogatives in the appropriations process; from the traditional reluctance to expand staff personnel, whether within the Appropriations Committee or as an external supplement, and from the various congressional reservations against assigning the GAO a budgetary pre-audit role. The proposed Joint Committee on the Budget also suffers from the basic limitation that many of the services it would provide the appropriations and legislative committees are essentially *permissive*. It would be a service committee. The appropriations committees retain their jurisdiction and power. Why would a chairman of one of the appropriations committees, who considered his own committee staff adequate for his work, accept the services of joint appropriations staff and the GAO?[67] The Joint Committee, as an alternative to the development of professional staff, faces the same limitation as other approaches—the education of members to the potential positive uses of professional staff assistance in congressional consideration of the budget. Three additional criticisms of the McClellan bill are worth noting.

1. *Experience with the Joint Committee concept—especially the Joint Committee on Atomic Energy —has created opposition, both within the executive and the legislature, to further extensions of the mechanism.* The Joint Committee on the Budget would have broad investigative powers paralleling in some regards the extraordinary powers of the JCAE.[68] The Budget Bureau has publicly opposed the provision in the bill that would permit the Joint Committee to obtain analytical, investigative, audit and other reports prepared by federal agencies other than the GAO. If this provision were strictly applied, confidential agency budget reports and Bureau of the Budget materials prepared for the President would be available to the committee—thereby, it is said, undermining the executive budget process. Extensive use of Budget Bureau personnel in executive sessions of the appropriations subcommittees would reduce their effectiveness within the executive branch, and might jeopardize the control of expenditures currently achieved by the Budget Bureau.

Related to the fear of possible inroads that a Joint Committee might make on executive prerogative is the more general argument that any measures that consolidate congressional committee structures or that develop cooperative links between the two Houses enhance congressional power and are therefore dangerous and undesirable.[69] This pro-executive argument is unlikely to carry much weight within Congress, however.

More serious objections come from within Congress itself. The Joint Committee would reduce the bicameral checks in the congressional review of the budget. It would combine two elements that play different roles in the budget game and would make the process of agency appeal considerably more

---

[67] As one appropriations staff member observed, "The Joint Budget Committee is just a holding company to get more help that we don't need. The majority of Appropriations members feel they have enough help already."

[68] See Green and Rosenthal, *op. cit.,* pp. 25-30, 266-73.

[69] James MacGregor Burns warns the would-be reformer that "the stronger the exertion of congressional power, the more conservative and isolationist will be our national policy." *Op. cit.,* p. 264.

difficult.[70] The close relationship the JCAE has developed with the Atomic Energy Commission is cited as reason to fear that a Joint Budget Committee would not be as critical of the budget and might "keep the lid on congressional debate." While some distinction between a joint legislative committee and a joint appropriations committee should be made, this fear points to a second problem.

2. *A Joint Appropriations Committee is apt to serve the needs of the respective appropriations committees rather than the membership of Congress.* While the need for meaningful interpretation and data on the budget extends to the full range of membership, the Joint Committee is designed explicitly to service the appropriations committees. Senator McClellan has assured his colleagues that his bill "will provide a means for obtaining more information by individual Members of Congress. . . . It will permit them to arrive at more informed judgments."[71] Others have expressed a fear that the Joint Committee, especially its ranking majority and minority members, would monopolize staff resources. The Joint Committee would only be "the appropriations committees wearing another hat." "You'd have the same men serving on both committees and they're unlikely to change a system that benefits them." "It would be like appointing the devil to investigate hell." As currently structured, the Joint Budget Committee proposal does not include adequate safeguards to insure that the services of the staff would be available to more than a few select members of the appropriations committees, it is said.

3. *The Joint Budget Committee is essentially a mechanical device that will only complicate the existing congressional machinery.* Several members interviewed seemed to feel that little good could come from a "mythical, theoretical coordinating committee" since the appropriations committees would retain responsibility and power in the system. A joint committee might mean just one more base to touch in an already complicated system. Executive agencies, already overburdened with the preparation of testimony and budget justifications for their four legislative and appropriations committees, would face needless additional harassment. This criticism admittedly has some justification, although it ignores some of the gains not immediately dependent on the

---

[70] Some fiscal conservatives see this as a positive gain by closing a major loophole in the system.

[71] *Congressional Record*, 88th Congress, 1st Session, January 25, 1963, p. 1099.

powers of the appropriations committees that supporters of the bill hope to realize.

*   *   *   *   *

Of the various proposals for reform considered, the Joint Budget Committee is in the best immediate position for passage. In the Eighty-eighth Congress it has had its perennial Senate endorsement as well as the support of the ranking minority member on House Appropriations, Congressman Jensen of Iowa. (John Taber, who formerly occupied that position, strongly opposed it.) If House sentiment for the measure grows, the new chairman of House Appropriations, Congressman Mahon, might not oppose it. Even if implemented, the Joint Committee would be largely limited to the appropriations side of the budgetary equation. Congress might

then move gradually to consolidate the staffs of the Joint Committee on the Budget and the Joint Committee on Internal Revenue Taxation, approaching the legislative budget by more gradual means.

Conclusion. The analysis of these five areas of congressional initiative has produced several, at times contradictory, explanations for congressional failure to implement reforms. The interrelationship of goals in the budgetary process and attitudes toward reform has been encountered again and again. These must now be considered explicitly as part of a strategy for budgetary reform. These five cases have also illustrated some of the structural givens in the congressional system as well as areas that may be susceptible to further change — also important considerations to a strategy for reform.

IV.

A STRATEGY FOR FISCAL REFORM—GOALS, LIMITATIONS, AND RECOMMENDATIONS

Up to this point we have raised but not faced the issue of underlying values and objectives in the budgetary process. The range of criticisms discussed and the arguments for and against specific reform proposals suggest the variety of interests and value preferences that are involved. Now as we approach the question of how Congress "should" reform itself, these value choices will have to be made explicit.

This study was undertaken specifically with a congressional focus. It recognizes that Congress as a body is a national institution with a vital role in the formulation of national policy. The function of Congress in representing local constituency interests has frequently been overemphasized to the exclusion of the broader role. It is assumed here that congressmen have considerable flexibility in developing a national perspective that is not inconsistent with the needs of representation.[1] A broader assumption is that it is in the national interest to strengthen Congress as a national institution. The underlying question of this study is "How can congressional power be used more responsibly and constructively in the determination of a national policy?"

The Choice of Goals

From this perspective four general objectives or goals are assumed to be appropriate for the congressional budgetary process. In harmony with these objectives, a number of recommendations for reforming the congressional budget system are presented.

Effecting economy and efficiency in government. The objective of providing services at the least cost to the taxpayer is at least as old as the Committee on Ways and Means. It provided part of the basis for

specific appropriations and the major impetus for a congressional post-audit. The problem of illegality of expenditures is no longer a major concern. Instead the *review* of agency spending has focused increasingly on improved management as the basis for efficient operation. (The assumption is made with regard to this objective that program decisions are already determined, i.e., that "allocation" is not included in the definition of "efficiency.")

Control of the growth and independent operation of the bureaucracy. Under the assumption that bureaucracy is not simply an instrument for implementing predetermined policies and that it has an independent life and interests of its own (including a natural tendency to expand), the need for congressional surveillance or "oversight" of the bureaucracy becomes a reasonable *corollary*. The added assumption is made that the President is frequently unable or not inclined to control the executive bureaucracy.[2] The appropriations process af-

---

[1] Recent studies of representation and constituency sanctions suggest that the congressman is relatively free in defining his role in the congressional system. See Raymond A. Bauer, Ithiel de Sola Pool, and Lewis A. Dexter, *American Business and Publicity Policy* (New York: Atherton Press, 1963), esp. pp. 403-24. Also Heinz Eulau, *et al.*, "The Role of the Representative: Some Empirical Observations on the Theory of Edmund Burke," *American Poliitcal Science Review,* September 1959, pp. 742-56. Ralph Huitt takes a more pessimistic view of the possibilities for bringing a unitary program out of a body "which is organized to respond to a multiplicity of pressures and demands." *Loc. cit.*, pp. 407-08, 426-27, 491-95.

[2] See David Truman's discussion of "The Ordeal of the Executive," *op. cit.*, esp. pp. 407-08, on the "decision to intervene." Also Peter Woll, *American Bureaucracy* (New York: W. W. Norton, 1963), pp. 145-72.

fords one of the most effective techniques for congressional oversight. Annual and multi-year authorizations afford another. Congressional oversight assumes the values of responsibility and representation,[3] and is considered here to be a valid objective in the congressional budget process. However, while oversight may contribute to the objective of efficiency, as it is extended it will limit the discretion of executive officials with the result of less efficient operation.

Review of overall fiscal policy. Congress should review the overall fiscal policy of the Federal Government proposed by the executive. It is assumed here that Congress has a vital role to play in the formulation of national fiscal policy. A corollary objective is *the right of "secondary initiative."* Congress not only has the power to amend or reorder priorities; it may also take the initiative where the executive has not. The role of the Joint Committee on Atomic Energy in promoting the Polaris nuclear submarine program against executive opposition is a persuasive example.[4] If Congress is to assume a positive role in broad issues of fiscal policy, it cannot rely simply on its four separate fiscal committees. It follows that this objective will require a new integrative mechanism.

This objective is related but not equivalent to a number of freqently stated objectives subsumed under the term "fiscal responsibility." Congress, via the appropriations process, has final control of the *level* of federal spending. Control of the level of spending can be defined in a number of ways. One of the most frequent formulations is the principle of the "balanced budget."[5] Others argue for more stringent reductions in spending with budgetary surpluses applied to reducing the national debt.[6] More limited forms of control would be the "balanced budget over the cycle" and keeping the national debt within a given percent of gross national product.

---

[3] *Supra,* pp. 25-26.

[4] The example and the term "secondary initiative" are from Congressman Chet Holifield.

[5] See for example H.R. 12394, 87th Congress, 2d Session, a bill "to provide that Federal expenditures shall not exceed Federal revenues, except in time of war or grave national emergency declared by the Congress."

[6] Congressman Morris Udall has proposed a U.S. Tax Commission which would adjust federal income taxes so that for each four-year period federal receipts would exceed federal expenditures by at least $4 billion. (H.R. 9816, 87th Congress, 2d Session.) H.R. 12734, 87th Congress, 1st Session, provided for a percentage of net budget receipts, up to 10 percent, to be devoted exclusively to the retirement of the public debt. S.J. Res. 29, 88th Congress, 1st Session (the Curtis-Byrd amendment) would amend the Constitution to provide for an annual reduction of the public debt "not less than $500,000,000."

These last definitions find less open support within Congress.

The objective assumed here is merely that Congress should consider overall fiscal policy. The level of spending (and revenues) achieved is a political decision that will be left to congressional determination.

Control as intelligent action based on adequate information. Congress should seek control with understanding of the impact of its actions at the program level. Control expressed simply through the mandating of expenditure reductions may be little more than the exercise of power. To attach an "economy" rider to an omnibus appropriations bill, to fix a ceiling on the national debt that effects similar economies, to enact continuing resolutions while deferring action on increased appropriations all are within the province of congressional power and may well serve to effectuate the congressional objective of controlling the level of federal spending. Yet they all represent an abdication of congressional power and responsibility in another sense. Congressional action is taken in ignorance. Unable or unwilling to make specific cuts via the normal appropria-

tions process, Congress resorts to crude or blunt uses of its power, not knowing what the effects of its actions will be on given programs— in effect giving the executive complete discretion in allocating the reduction. One defense of such congressional action is that Congress must reduce the enormous burden of calculating the budget, and that meat-axe cuts are a necessary aid to calculation.[7] If Congress had provided itself with more adequate staff to inform itself of the specifics of the budget and to gain a better understanding of the operation of agency programs, this argument might be more convincing. The assumption is made here that Congress has not developed its staff optimally to gain knowledge for informed action. Congressmen, both in their committee capacities and as individual members, do not have adequate information in usable, digested form.

Improved information alone, however, will not insure more effective congressional control and coordination. But it is an essential prerequisite to increased rationality in the budget process.[8]

*   *   *   *   *

---

[7] *Supra,* pp. 28-29.

[8] Admittedly the psychology of budget-cutting drives is not concerned with impact on specific programs. Given the nature of the congressional system such behavior will always carry political advantage for some participants. This fact of political life, however, does not obviate the objective of greater rationality.

Four *general* objectives or goals have been defined as appropriate to a "national" congressional role in the budgetary process: (1) economy and efficiency in governmental operations, (2) surveillance or oversight of the bureaucracy, (3) review of overall fiscal policy (with the right of "secondary initiative") and (4) control as intelligent action based on adequate information. Some recommendations are implicit in these objectives. But before they are stated, a realistic assessment of the limitations to meaningful reform is necessary.

The Limitation to Reform

A basic assumption in our approach is that wholesale renovation of the congressional budgetary machinery (i.e., the congressional system) is unrealistic and that further efforts in this direction are likely to prove fruitless. The basic characteristics of the system described above are assumed as given: the dual structure of authorization and appropriation, the committee system based on norms of specialization and reciprocity, and the allocation and reciprocal expectation of roles in the budgetary process. While it would be foolish to attribute the property of immutability to any of these the probability of a major change is sufficently small to justify ignoring it.

A further assumption follows. The most realistic approach to congressional reform, in this area and elsewhere, is evolutionary development of reform "inclinations" already present in the congressional system and its membership.[9] It should be clear by now that such inclinations toward fiscal reform do exist, that they have not been adequately articulated or formulated in practical reforms, and that they have often worked at cross purposes to each other. A number of these inclinations are toward developing a more effective national role for Congress. That is to say there already exists within Congress substantial sentiment to move in the direction of the objectives we have assumed appropriate to a "national" congressional role in the budgetary process.[10] The prospects for reform are, of course, enhanced by the existence of such attitudes.

[9] Wildavsky concludes that "small, incremental changes, proceeding in a pragmatic fashion of trial and error could proceed as before without benefit of theory; but this is not the kind of change with which the literature on budgeting is generally concerned." "Political Implications of Budgetary Reform," *loc. cit.,* p. 190. The approach adopted here attempts to apply theory and an understanding of the system to gradual *but* directed reform.

[10] See Davidson, Kovenock, and O'Leary, *op. cit.,* Appendix B, "Congressional Attitudes Toward Congressional Reorganization," pp. 6-12.

Several terrain features in the congressional landscape[11] impose limitations to reform beyond the general characteristics of the system already noted. First is the fourfold division of the budget among the four great fiscal committees— House Ways and Means, House Appropriations, Senate Finance, and Senate Appropriations. Few members would advocate consolidating these either within the two Houses or through joint committees, or removing the authority over revenues and appropriations from them to a super fiscal committee superimposed upon them. Bicameralism, the increasing congressional workload, and the differences in specialized knowledge and training required are all cited as justifications of the existing division.[12] A joint committee, which many members still feel is necessary, would have to build on these realities of power, not as a potential competitor to the fiscal committees. The coordination it would seek to effect would be horizontal and not vertical—the latter implying hierarchy and an element of coercion. We should note the congressional disinclination to concentrate too much power at crucial points of decision within the system.

Second among these terrain features is the preeminence of the House Committee on Appropriations within the system, both due to its position and roles in the appropriations process and to the congressional inclination to concentrate on the expenditure rather than the revenue side of the budget. Effective control of spending will continue to be focused within House Appropriations and its subcommittees. Reforms to develop more adequate information for congressional action and to provide more adequate professional staff should be related insofar as possible to this reality.

Third, while the House Appropriations Committee remains the key element, the inevitable tensions between it and the legislative committees and between it and the membership of the House impose real limitations to admissible increases in its power. Reforms such as the omnibus appropriations bill which put the membership at a disadvantage to the committee are not likely to be accepted. This suggests

---

[11] The analogy is from Bertram Gross, *op. cit.*, p. 166.

[12] Wallace, *op. cit.*, pp. 153-54. A good case can be made for a further reduction of the workload allocated to Ways and Means. Most of the major legislation of the 87th Congress was referred to the Committee (tax revision and reform, trade expansion, medicare, welfare reforms, unemployment compensation, the debt ceiling, etc.). This was an important yet often overlooked reason for the extended sessions of this Congress.

the need for some balance between the committee and the House, particularly in providing budgetary information and professional staff assistance.

Finally, it should be clear that any reforms that are introduced will only be as effective as the Congress makes them. Revising the congressional calendar, creating a new joint coordinating committee, providing Congress the necessary staff and information to make intelligent judgments on the budget, etc., will not in themselves give Congress the effective role it seeks. The basic limitation is one of self-education and self-discipline.

These realistic limitations may be formidable, but they do not necessarily close the door to meaningful congressional reform. The question becomes: "What reforms can be suggested that are directed toward the stated objectives, that accord with congressional inclinations for change, and that do not present a clear and present danger to any of the basic interests within the system?"

Recommendations for Reforming the Congressional Budgetary System

The conclusions that emerge from this study are not comprehensive in the sense of providing answers for all the issues raised in the course of the paper. They are not developed as full legislative proposals. But they are advanced as suggestions, for consideration, of practicable means of better equipping the Congress for responsible use of its proper powers in certain important areas of budget control and fiscal policy formulation.

1. *Congress should establish a Joint Committee on Fiscal Policy.*[13]

Profiting from the experience and criticisms of the Joint Committee on the Legislative Budget and the proposed Joint Committee on the Budget (McClellan), the new committee should meet the following specifications. It should be streamlined in membership with repre-

[13] A similar but less flexible instrument is Arthur Smithies' proposal for a Joint Budget Policy Committee. The leadership of both political parties would be "strongly represented." The new committee also retains the concurrent resolution of the 1946 Act but at a later stage in the process, and the concept of the omnibus appropriations bill. *Op. cit.,* pp. 192-97. The Committee for Economic Development has recommended a Joint Budget Policy Conference (without the concurrent resolution provision) whose major functions would be "study of current fiscal policy and consideration of the long-run effects of the budget." Research and Policy Committee of the Committee for Economic Development, *Control of Federal Government Expenditures: A Statement on National Policy* (New York: CED, 1955), pp. 15-16.

sentation from the four fiscal committees.[14] (Total membership, including representatives from any additional committees, should not exceed 20.) Members need not be the most senior members of their respective committees but should be selected on the basis of experience and interest. They should be men who are "listened to" on their committees—men who have already mastered the art of congressional influence.[15] The strengths and weaknesses of another major congressional experiment — the Joint Economic Committee — can be traced in large part to this factor.

The Joint Committee should not be required to submit a formal legislative budget for congressional enactment. At most it should develop budgetary guidelines to assist the fiscal committees (guidelines that probably would be kept confidential). Primarily, it should provide a forum for continuing congressional consideration of the budget, changing economic and political assumptions on which the budget is based, and the status of authorizations, appropriations, and revenue measures.

Its functions should be advisory and informational and should probably include responsibility for several of the proposals listed below. It should be adequately staffed to carry out the functions assigned to it. The temptation must be avoided of giving the committee unrealistic objectives that invite disappointment.

The utilities of a Joint Committee on Fiscal Policy—apart from specific functions it might handle— are several. It would provide a far more effective channel for communication than now exists informally between the Houses and the fiscal committees. This is not an insignificant gain if one considers how infrequently members of various committees testify before other committees on questions concerning the budget. The committee would also provide a means for Congress to express its sentiments on broad fiscal policy where it now speaks with several voices or frequently not at all. Again the Joint Economic Committee provides an example. Its reports and staff studies command attention within the executive and the academic com-

---

[14] Other committees that might be included (perhaps on a nonvoting or ex-officio basis) are Government Operations, Banking and Currency, and Joint Economic.

[15] See Congressman Miller's description of congressional power, Baker ed., *op. cit.,* pp. 104-06. ". . . the congressman who consults privately with shrewdness, who has just come from a closed meeting with somebody with information to impart, who works quietly underground, will wind up in the donjon with the prize. He will, in the course of time, exert influence. He will be asked for his opinion. In a profession which makes much of handing out advice, it is being asked for it that is the greatest jewel."

munity in general, while to a lesser extent educating the membership of Congress to broader economic issues. The JEC has made possible a meaningful dialogue between the President and Congress on the state of the nation's economy. Finally a Joint Committee would provide the best basis for developing information on the budget for use by the full membership of Congress. The chances of its staff being monopolized by one or two of the fiscal committees is less than would be the case with an increase of regular committee staff or a joint appropriations staff. A joint committee could give Congress a continuing picture of the budget that it now lacks.

The example of the JEC may invite the further comparison and criticism, that such an "advisory" committee has little if any immediate impact on the legislative process. The committee has been reluctant to press its views on economic policy before the legislative committees responsible for economic policy decisions. The McClellan committee, however, would be enjoined to receive information from and to make reports and recommendations to the legislative committees. Similar provisions could be incorporated under a Joint Committee on Fiscal Policy.

A Joint Committee on Fiscal Policy could be established in one of three ways: (1) as a new Joint Committee, perhaps via amendment of section 138 of the Legislative Reorganization Act (the McClellan approach), (2) by expanding the membership and functions of the Joint Economic Committee,[16] or (3) in two steps, by establishing a Joint Appropriations Committee with staff and then merging it with the Joint Committee on Internal Revenue Taxation.

2. Congress should exert more control at the authorization stage of the budgetary process.

Congress must give more consideration to the time dimension of expenditure. Instead of viewing the budget as largely inflexible due to prior commitments, Congress should focus its attention on the new authorizations and those long-term or "open" authorizations that may be subject to revision. The trend toward annual and multi-year authorizations has meant greater congressional control in the latter case but new authorizations remain a problem (especially when one recognizes that annual authorization may be a deliberate effort on the part of the legislative committees

---

[16] An alternative suggested by the CED, *op. cit.,* p. 16.

to increase appropriations).[17] Some additional external constraint is required.

In 1956, Congress enacted into law a requirement that cost information be included in all agency reports to congressional committees on proposed legislation. In theory, as one congressional study states, "each report on a pending or proposed bill contains the probable cost or savings attributable to the legislative proposal over each year of the first five years of operation." Also included are the estimated maximum additional man-years of employment and expenditures for personal services.[18] In fact, this provision has not been adequate. Cost information submitted by the agencies has been uneven and congressional committee staff have often been unable to give the data a searching review. When one adds to this the tendency of agencies and sympathetic committees to underestimate costs in the budget game— a common strategy—this approach to the control of authorizations appears to have limited effectiveness.

Accordingly several members of Congress have introduced resolutions that would require every report from a committee (other than Appropriations) to include estimated appropriation or fund requirements for new programs for each of the first five fiscal years they are to be in effect. A comparison of committee estimates with corresponding recommendations from the executive branch would also be required.[19] Another resolution would require the inclusion of similar cost estimates in the executive budget as submitted.[20]

Congress should act to insure it has as adequate cost data as can be reasonably expected on requests for new program authorizations. Its legislative committees should be adequately staffed to collect and evaluate such data from the agencies. Staff personnel from a Joint Committe on Fiscal Policy or the GAO could be made available on request to the committees to assist them in setting up procedures

---

[17] This was probably the intent of annual authorization for the NASA budget. Frye and Saloma, *op. cit.,* pp. 17-21. See also Green and Rosenthal, *op. cit.,* chap, v, "Authorizing Techniques and Decision-Making," esp. pp. 170-71. The extension of annual authorization to the Coast Guard in the current session is the most recent example.

[18] *Financial Management in the Federal Government, op. cit.,* p. 137. Previously the Bureau of the Budget had compiled such information informally.

[19] H.Res. 185, 88th Congress, 1st Session (Judge Howard Smith).

[20] H.J. Res. 294, 88th Congress, 1st Session (Judge Howard Smith). Another technique for relating individual budget decisions to the overall state of federal finances is suggested by Weidenbaum, *op. cit.,* pp. 72-77.

for cost analysis and projection. To ensure compliance, the Rules Committee could legitimately refuse to consider or grant rules for bills that were not accompanied by full cost information.

This reform would permit more intelligent congressional action at one of the critical points of control in the congressional budget process.

3. *The appropriations committees should provide for a more integrated review of the budget.*

Reform at the authorization level is not enough. The aggregate of individually meritorious programs is still bound to add up to "too much." Further screening is provided by the individual subcommittees of Appropriations but the full committee exerts minimal control.[21] The legislative budget and omnibus appropriations bill both suggest techniques that could be adopted on a regular basis at the full committee level.

At the beginning of the session the Appropriations Committee, with the consultation of the Joint Committee on Fiscal Policy, should define a set of flexible budgetary guidelines, a modest effort toward a legislative budget. The appropriations committees should each set up a coordinating subcommittee, composed of the chairmen of the various subcommittees, which would recommend appropriations ceilings to the subcommittees. In the experience with the consolidated appropriations bill, this "steering committee" did not have the power to amend subcommittee bills but it could refer them back to the subcommittee with recommendations. The executive budget process functions with a similar set of preliminary estimates, and if the appropriations target figures are treated as flexible and kept confidential within the steering committee the process should be feasible. The appropriations committees have experimented with procedures like this before. They should now establish them on a regular basis.

Reinstitution of the consolidated appropriations bill—a logical step in this process—should be approached cautiously, perhaps not until staff and budget information services for the membership are improved.

4. *The appropriations committees should increase their staffs to develop adequate information for appropriations decisions.*

Effective congressional control at the appropriations stage ultimately will depend upon the thoroughness of the work the appropriations committees and their staffs do. The committees are free to develop several alternative staff sources: regu-

---

[21] Fenno, *op. cit.*, p. 315.

lar professional committee staff, investigatory staff, joint appropriations staff, the GAO, etc. They are free to set the rules governing the use of staff personnel. Staff resources external to the committee's control can serve useful functions (see recommendation 7), but they cannot, barring revolutionary shifts of power in the appropriations process, replace the budget review and analysis that occurs at the appropriations subcommittee level.

Ideally appropriations staff members should meet several qualifications. They should meet high professional standards and receive commensurate salaries. They should develop a thorough acquaintance with the agency budgets to which they are assigned. Frequent rotation of regular committee staff or excessive reliance on temporary investigative staff are accordingly not desirable. By virtue of their position in the legislative branch they will have to depend to a considerable degree on information developed by the agencies and Budget Bureau. They cannot ·approximate the access or accumulated first hand knowledge of the Bureau's budget examiners. But they should be in a position to troubleshoot or spot-

check agency estimates.[22] We have already noted the quasi-advocate role that the Bureau may assume. Add to this the fact of a political executive directing the formulation of the budget and an appreciation of the size and complexity of modern bureaucracy and the case for an independent staff responsible to the appropriations committees is clear.

Two specific reforms are suggested. First, the number of regular professional staff employees should be increased. The 1946 recommendation of four staff members per subcommittee (to be reassigned according to work load) is a reasonable start. The minority should have at least one staff member responsible to it on each subcommitte. The bulk of the committee staff personnel should serve members on request, without regard to party affiliation or seniority. The natural tendency for subcommittee chairmen and ranking minority members to receive a disproportionate amount of staff service available to the subcommittee can be partially corrected by a moderate increase in staff, but may better be approached through the adoption of committee rules spelling out staffing procedures.[23]

---

[22] The long tenure of appropriations staff, like that of many members of the appropriations committees, affords them a knowledge through experience that their younger Budget Bureau counterparts may not yet have.

[23] Some members interviewed felt that more attention should be given to using appropriations staff outside of congressional sessions.

Second, the current restrictions on the use of the special investigative staff members greatly reduce their utility to the committee membership and should be relaxed to permit closer association with staff personnel. Subcommittees should be able to redefine the terms of reference and objectives of investigations as they unfold. Such subcommittee guidance of special investigations should increase the effectiveness of investigative staff work. Furthermore, investigative staff personnel should be free to brief the subcommittees on findings, answer members' questions, and sit in on agency hearings on request of the subcommittees.

The assumption is made in both these recommendations that potential gains in committee effectiveness far outweigh the traditional fears of increased staffing. The further assumption is made that increased staffing is necessary if the appropriations function is to be exercised responsibly. The burden of calculation the committee faces is a persuasive argument for more effective staffing arrangements, not a justification for time-saving techniques such as meat-axe cuts and the incremental approach to budgeting.

5. *The appropriations committees should make more effective use of the expenditure analysis and review accomplished by the Committees on Government Operations and the GAO.*

The appropriations committees can effect better integration at another level — expenditure review. The House Appropriations Committee has made increasing use of GAO audits and investigations in recent years. However, the communication between its members and staff employees and their counterparts on Government Operations, the committees immediately responsible for expenditure review, is limited.[24]

As financial control has focused more on improvements in management and organization and less on specific items of expenditure — a trend reflected in the changing orientation of the GAO—the appropriations committees should tap the experience and knowledge of both the GAO and the Committees on Government Operations. Witnesses should be invited to testify before appropriations subcommittees on a regular basis. There is some sentiment for a more formal coordination of the appropriations and review functions but this might lead to an unnecessary proliferation of

---

[24] See Clapp, *op. cit.*, p. 219. Also Kofmehl, *op. cit.*, chap. x, "Interstaff Relations," esp. p. 147.

committees.[25] Alternatively the suggested Joint Committee on Fiscal Policy might through its reports and recommendations reinforce the position of the GAO and Government Operations, especially with reference to the authorizing committees.

6. *Congress should provide means for better-informed partisan debate on the budget.*

On the assumption that the budget will continue to be a subject for partisan debate, Congress should facilitate intelligent, informed discussion between the parties. This can be accomplished through a better distribution of budgetary information to the general membership. More specifically it means providing the minority spokesmen—the minority members of the fiscal committees—with adequate professional staff facilities. House Appropriations affords a particular problem. Each ranking minority member on the subcommittees receives an allowance for clerk hire sufficient to hire a secretary or junior staff member but insufficient to retain a senior professional staff assistant.[26] The minority staff employees are not permitted to sit in appropriations hearings and as a result frequently become absorbed into the members' office staffs. The House Republican Appropriations (Bow) Task Force had to recruit additional voluntary assistance from the minority staff of the Senate Appropriations Committee and from outside the Congress during the Eighty-eighth Congress.[27]

The Bow Task Force operated with its own set of confidential appropriation targets in a parallel fashion to the steering committee included in recommendation 3. Although it is too early to predict the permanence of the minority appropriations task force, this might well be a development that will contribute to integrated congressional consideration of the budget.[28]

---

[25] Arthur Smithies suggests a formal expenditure review process by Appropriations and Government Operations jointly in addition to the annual appropriations review. *Op. cit.*, pp. 178-83. Wilmerding proposes a Joint Committee on Public Accounts. See his testimony, *Hearings: Organization and Operation of Congress, op. cit.*, pp. 495-504.

[26] *Supra,* p. 46, n. 21.

[27] In the case of Senate Appropriations, a minority staff works closely with ranking minority members in preparing for pre-mark-up conferences between the subcommittee chairmen and the respective ranking minority members.

[28] The case can be made that increased debate between the parties would contribute to more strife and "irresponsible" party actions at the expense of Appropriations Committee unity and continuity of policy. The assumption of this recommendation, however, is that there are legitimate roles for party in the legislative process which can be improved without disrupting the congressional system.

7. Congress should develop a Budget Information Service as one of the functions of a Joint Committee on Fiscal Policy.

Congress does not have a current, authoritative picture of the budget as it passes through the congressional budget cycle. It initially receives the President's budget which is later updated in the mid-year review. Agency presentations are available in appropriations hearings. Committee reports and the *Congressional Record* provide further information. But at a given stage in the session it is extremely difficult to determine what Congress has done to that date with the executive budget. What is the status of the various appropriation bills? What changes have Ways and Means and Senate Finance made in the revenue provisions requested by the President? What have the findings of the Joint Committee on Internal Revenue Taxation been in regard to the revenue estimates? This kind of information would be purely factual with respect to relevant congressional actions and findings. It would not require a large investigative staff. In view of this it is surprising that Congress has not already moved to set up a clearing house service on the budget. As a general rule Congress should not needlessly duplicate the informational services provided by the executive (the Budget Bureau has made numerous revisions in the budget document and explanatory materials that accompany it to make them more intelligible and serviceable to the Congress).[29] But, in this instance, the information is clearly internal to Congress and should be a congressional staff responsibility.

The utility of cost information at the authorization stage (recommendation 2) would similarly be increased if it were integrated into periodically revised congressional reports on the status of the budget. Congress should have at all times as complete a picture as possible of the budget and of the effects its actions are likely to have. These are modest reforms that are essential to any significant increase in congressional control of the budget.

All of these information services are provided under the proposed McClellan Joint Committee. They are logically assignable to a Joint Committee on Fiscal Policy. There are two additional information services that might be considered in a

---

[29] See testimony of Charles L. Schultze, Assistant Director, Bureau of the Budget, Subcommittee on Economic Statistics, Joint Economic Committee, *Hearings: The Federal Budget as an Economic Document,* 88th Congress, 1st Session, 1963, esp. pp. 149-58.

package of reforms. First, objective interpretative analyses of the budget, perhaps broken down to correspond with the appropriation bills, perhaps on selected aspects of the budget, might be prepared for the use of individual members. These analyses could sharpen the major policy decisions implicit or explicit in the President's budget. They could be cross referenced to other budgetary documents, committee hearings, GAO investigations, for the member who wants to dig deeper. They would be, in effect, condensations of committee hearings, tailored to the use of the member. Ideally, committee reports should serve this function, but the general stance of the House Appropriations Committee—the presentation of a united front to the House without minority reports—would appear to bar this alternative. For similar reasons an expansion of the professional staff of the committee to develop analyses for the use of the membership might prove disappointing. A Joint Committee Staff, supplemented by the GAO, may be the only feasible alternative. One qualification should be noted. The type of analyses suggested here should not be construed to be a substitute for the budget review and analysis performed by the House Appropriations Committee. It would be a supplementary service provided for the general membership. The intent would be to provide a means of raising the general level of understanding and debate. Nothing will replace hard work and application in arriving at the detailed component decisions that go into making the budget. As a rule, the individual member will still have to defer to his colleagues on the committee who have had the time and have taken the effort to do their "homework."

A second suggested reform pertaining to the availability of information to the Congress would be applicable to the form of the budget document itself, a proper concern of the Bureau of the Budget rather than a congressional staff office. The budget document serves as the basis for decision making by the Congress.[30] It is now the only common point of reference for the fiscal committees and subcommittees of Congress. A recent study of the federal budget document by the Subcommittee on Economic Statistics of the Joint Economic Committee concluded that the budget in its present form was "out moded." Extensive

---

[30] Subcommittee on Economic Statistics, Joint Economic Committee, *Report: The Federal Budget as an Economic Document,* 88th Congress, 1st Session, 1963, p. 2. See also comments by Congressman Thomas B. Curtis, *Hearings: The Federal Budget as an Economic Document, op. cit.,* p. 194.

revisions in format and content were suggested to facilitate the analysis of federal policies. The subcommittee report noted that—

> . . . the essence of budget decision making is a comparison between alternative policies. If the information on each of these alternative policies is to be found in diverse and relatively obscure sources, the budgetary comparisons are much more difficult.[31]

To resolve "the dilemma of budgetary reform" (i.e., the simultaneous demand for greater simplicity and more detail), the subcommittee made several recommendations, one of which bears directly on the utility of budgetary information. The budget, it suggested, should be presented on a program basis *but* with a program classification so based on an overall index system that appropriations requests could still be made on an agency basis by the functions performed. Cross indexing on a functional program basis would enable all users of the budget, not the least Congress, to determine the types of activities in which the Federal Government is engaged and the dollar significance of these activities. The subcommittee cited the

example of the appropriations for education in 1961 which were postponed when it was discovered that "educational activities were carried on by such a host of agencies, offices, divisions, bureaus, and other bodies that no one in the Government really knew what the total figures were or what the educational end result or accomplishment had been."[32] Information on this basis, the report concluded, is "not only relevant for congressional decision making but is also equally relevant for the agency decision making that presumably underlies proposals to the Congress."[33]

The major objection that has been raised against functional cross indexing is the problem of definition. Is the school-lunch program, for instance, to be included under education, agriculture (surplus disposal), or welfare activities? The budget cannot easily be resolved into clearcut functional components. The Budget Bureau has been approaching this problem gradually. "Special analyses" on important aspects of federal activity—research and development, grants-in-aid to state and local governments, expenditures for statistical programs, etc. — have been added to the

---

[31] *Report: The Federal Budget as an Economic Document, op. cit.,* p. 15.
[32] *Ibid.,* p. 7.
[33] *Ibid.,* p. 14.

budget. The Bureau is also studying the development of an integrated classification code for the budget, and the possibilities for increasing the use of automatic data processing equipment.[34] Ultimately it may be possible to develop a full series of special analyses from the current mass of budget data. These analyses would be nonadditive but they could provide useful partial perspectives on a government-wide basis. In the congressional budget process, they would afford a broader view of governmental spending than is currently available to the highly specialized appropriations subcommittees.[35]

Additional changes in the budget document have been proposed which are not discussed at length here. Several deal with the methods of budgetary accounting. One proposal would convert the budget from its current basis of new obligational authority (NOA, i.e., the sum of new authorizations to incur obligations—place orders, award contracts, receive services, etc.) to an accrued expenditure basis.[36] Congressional control, now limited to the control of NOA, could then be extended to actual expenditure ceilings for a given year. "Expenditure control" goes beyond the provision of information on an expenditure basis. It would impose a new discipline on agency programming, and reduce the flexibility or discretionary range in the timing of expenditures.[37] While Congress could enforce this type of expenditure control, more modest informational reforms in the budget document should probably be attempted first. The Bureau of the Budget should be encouraged to develop improvements already underway and to continue discussions with the Joint Economic and the major fiscal committees on further changes in the format of the budget document.

[34] *Hearings: The Federal Budget as an Economic Document, op. cit.,* p. 156.

[35] Several members and staff interviewed expressed the view that the executive was unlikely to implement an effective cross indexing system for congressional use for fear "it would open a Pandora's box." The executive by implication would prefer to keep the appropriations subcommittees within their narrow fields.

[36] For a discussion of progress toward annual accrued expenditure limitations—a recommendation of the second Hoover Commission—and the objections raised by the House Appropriations Committee, especially in regard to the device of "contract authority," see *Financial Management in the Federal Government, op. cit.,* pp. 56-60, 98-110.

[37] See Congressman Curtis' discussion of "expenditure control." *Hearings: The Federal Budget as an Economic Document, op. cit.,* pp. 194-203. For a full definition of the various budget concepts see Subcommittee on Economic Statistics, Joint Economic Committee, *Joint Committee Print: The Federal Budget as an Economic Budget,* 87th Congress, 2d Session, 1962, Pt. II, "Budget Concepts."

8. *Congress should improve the scheduling of the congressional budget process.*

The delay of appropriation bills well beyond the beginning of the fiscal year has become a chronic problem that merits congressional attention. We have already noted the trend toward annual authorization as a major factor. Assuming that this trend is not reversed, Congress will soon have to give consideration to changes in its schedule or subject the executive agencies to severe planning difficulties.

As a first step, Congress should accept the year-round session with scheduled recesses as normal. It is inconsistent to aim for a July 1 adjournment and press at the same time for a meaningful legislative budget with adequate review at the authorization stage.[38] On the basis of a year-round session, the congressional leadership should then project a schedule for authorization and appropriation bills. The current pattern might be regularized with major authorization bills (NASA, foreign aid, etc.) to be completed by the first of September; appropriation bills between then and adjournment. This would in effect shift the fiscal year back six months to coincide with the calendar year, while adding six months to the period of budget formulation and congressional review (see Figure I).

An alternative and preferable course would be, again on the basis of a full-year session, to advance the authorization phase from the beginning of the session to the previous September for programs requiring annual authorization. Most authorizations could then be completed by April or May; appropriations, by July first. In either case the executive budget process will have to make adjustments to accommodate the expanded congressional activity. A six-month span for the congressional budget process, confined at one end by the budget submission, at the other by the new fiscal year, is no longer a realistic assumption.

A Postscript on Expectations

The strategy of reform suggested above is essentially a low "cost" strategy in that it does not present an immediate challenge to the basic elements of the congressional power structure. We have assumed that a high cost strategy has little likelihood of success without an unforeseeable change in the climate of congressional opinion. It does not follow, however, that the gains that could be realized from the suggested

---

[38] An alternative to an extended session would be a shift to a full committee work week (as opposed to the current Tuesday-Thursday mode of operation).

reforms would be inconsequential.

Essentially, what we have done has been to take the basic power structure of Congress as given and to seek to rationalize it. In a system characterized by dispersed centers of power rather than hierarchy and command, we have emphasized steps to facilitate inter-unit bargaining, negotiation, and compromise. The recommendations for a Joint Committee on Fiscal Policy and a Budget Information Service attempt to institutionalize communication and information functions that are not being met by the current budgetary system.

The reforms that have been presented assume that a need for rationalization at this level exists, and is perceived by a growing number of members of Congress. If this assessment is correct we can expect marginal, yet cumulative, gains in our objectives of economy, oversight, overall policy review, and budgetary control. A serious congressional effort to rationalize its procedures, in itself, should also realize the gains of increased public prestige and a greater sense of congressional efficacy.

*   *   *   *   *

The reforms suggested here develop a common theme. Congress should exercise its constitutional powers responsibly by accepting the full implications of a national role. This means equipping Congress and its committees with the means for informed judgment and intelligent action.

Congress alone bears the responsibility for the failure to develop the reforms of 1921 and 1946. Further improvements in the federal budget process now await its approval. As Congress begins a new period of introspection, it would do well to consider its disappointing experience with fiscal reform and the still unrealized potential for effective congressional action.

FIGURES

Figure I.   Major Steps in the Budget Process[1]
(Illustrative dates — Fiscal Year 1965)

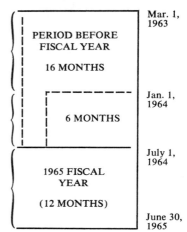

FORMULATION OF EXECUTIVE BUDGET

CONGRESSIONAL ACTION ON
APPROPRIATIONS (AND REVENUE
MEASURES)*

EXECUTION OF ENACTED BUDGET**

PERIOD BEFORE
FISCAL YEAR

16 MONTHS

6 MONTHS

1965 FISCAL
YEAR

(12 MONTHS)

Mar. 1,
1963

Jan. 1,
1964

July 1,
1964

June 30,
1965

* If action is not completed by June 30, Congress enacts continuing resolution.
** Financial data for fiscal year available by following September 30.

APPROXIMATE TIMING OF MAJOR STEPS IN THE BUDGET PROCESS:

Formulation

March 1963   Agencies determine policies and broad guidelines for estimates.

Bureau of the Budget (BOB) develops economic assumptions and fiscal projections (in cooperation with the Treasury and Council of Economic Advisers).

April-May 1963   BOB (after discussing budgetary outlook with President) issues instructions for spring program review.

Spring program review—major agencies submit information on programs, policy issues, and budgetary projections for budget year and succeeding three years.

June 1963   BOB discusses program developments with agency heads. Then compiles total expenditure estimates, compares with revenue estimates, develops recommendations for President on fiscal policy.

President discusses with Budget Director *general budget policy,* major program issues, projections.
Establishes *planning figures* for annual budget.

July-Sept. 30, 1963 Agencies allocate planning figures to programs. Coordinate and compile *detailed estimates.*

[1] Extracted from materials prepared by the Bureau of the Budget, Executive Office of the President, July 1962. The Budget Bureau graphs used for Figure I and Figure III have been reproduced in an Appendix to Aaron Wildavsky, *The Politics of the Budgetary Process* (Boston: Little, Brown and Co., 1964), pp. 194-99. For a fuller definition of the budget terminology, see Murray L. Weidenbaum, *Federal Budgeting: The Choice of Government Programs* (Washington: American Enterprise Institute, 1964).

Sept.-Oct 1963	Agencies submit formal estimates for annual budget.
	BOB makes general and technical analysis of estimates. Holds *hearings* with agency representatives. Reexamines assumptions . . .
Nov. 1963	*Presidential* review and *decision* on agency amounts.
Dec.-Jan. 1964	Agencies *revise estimates* to conform with presidential decision.
	BOB again reviews assumptions, drafts budget message, *prepares budget* with summary tables.
	President revises and approves *budget message, transmits recommended budget* to Congress.

Congressional Action

| Jan.-July 1, 1964 | CONGRESSIONAL ACTION ON APPROPRIATIONS (see Figures II, III) |

Execution

May-July 1964	On approval of appropriation bill, *appropriation warrant*, drawn by Treasury and countersigned by General Accounting Office (GAO), is forwarded to agency.
	Agencies *revise operating budget* in view of approved appropriations, prepare request for apportionment.
	BOB makes *apportionment* by June 10 or within 30 days after approval of appropriations. May "reserve" funds for contingencies, savings, or developments subsequent to enactment. (May reapportion at any time.)
Control over Funds Continuous	Agencies *allot* apportioned funds to various programs and activities, submit summarized financial plans and progress reports to BOB. *Obligate money.* Receive and use goods and services.
	BOB analyzes reports, prepares progress reports for President, comparing expenditures with financial plans.
Expenditure of Funds as Bills Become Payable	Agencies prepare and certify vouchers and invoices for payment.
	Treasury issues checks and *reports on expenditures* in Monthly Treasury Statement and Treasury Bulletin.
Management Appraisal and Independent Audit Periodic	GAO performs *independent audit*. "Settles" accounts of certifying and disbursing officers, makes *reports to Congress*.
	Agencies review compliance with established policies, procedures, and regulations. Evaluate accomplishment of program plans and effectiveness of management and operations.
	BOB makes informal review of agency operations. Conducts organization and management studies within executive branch.

Figure II. Components of the Congressional Budget Process. (Idealized)

Congressional Activity	Congressional Agent(s)	Relationship to Overall Budget Process	Relationship to Congressional Budget Process
Authorization	Legislative committees of House, Senate Conference committees	Receive, consider, and act upon legislative proposals in the program of the President or from other sources. Make broad program and policy decisions. Recommend authorizations of upper limits (in terms of time and/or amount) of spending.	Authorization must precede appropriations. General or open ended authorizations reduce the involvement of the legislative committees in the budget process. Annual authorization requires legislative committee approval each year before appropriations can be enacted.
Appropriations	Appropriations subcommittes and committees of House, Senate Conference committees	Receive President's budget in mid-January. Receive written justifications of agency estimates. Hold hearings. Appropriate funds within the limits of congressional authorization.	Require prior congressional authorization. Usually initiated by House Committee on Appropriations. Senate Committee normally serves an appellate function. Provide funds to implement policies and programs authorized by Congress.
Revenue Measures	House Committee on Ways and Means Senate Finance Committee Conference committees Joint Committee on Internal Revenue Taxation (Staff)	Receive President's budget in mid-January. Receive, consider and recommend congressional actions on revenue measures proposed by the President.	Initiated by House Committee on Ways and Means. Considered independently from appropriations—within the general framework of the Executive budget. (Coordination at a general, informal level.)

Figure II. (continued)

Congressional Activity	Congressional Agent(s)	Relationship to Overall Budget Process	Relationship to Congressional Budget Process
Economic Analysis Coordination of Economic Policy	Joint Economic Committee	Receives, reviews, and reports on the Economic Report of the President (on the state of the economy; economic policy recommendations: fiscal policy, measures to promote full employment, price stability, economic growth, etc.). Makes independent studies and economic analysis periodically.	No formal association with authorization, appropriation and revenue decisions of the Congress. Serves an educational or informational role within the Congress (overlapping membership with various House and Senate committees).
Expenditure Review	Committee on Government Operations of House, Senate Appropriations subcommittees and committees, House, Senate Legislative committees of House, Senate Joint Committee on Non-Essential Expenditures	Receive reports and audits from GAO, act on selected reports. Initiate independent committee investigations Review agency performance during hearings on budget estimates. Investigatory staffs function with government-wide jurisdiction. Perform continuous process of "oversight" or surveillance of agency activities.	Committees on Government Operations may recommend action to the appropriation or legislative committees. Agency review generates new inputs to the authorization and appropriations processes.

Figure III. Relationship of Congressional Authorization–Appropriations Processes[1]
—Assuming requirement of annual authorization—

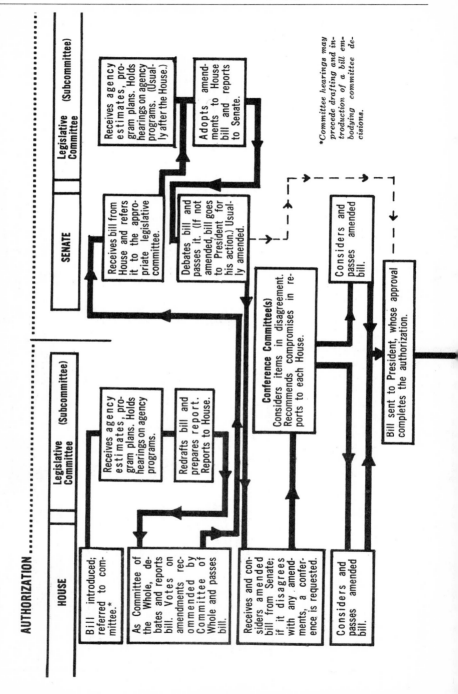

Committee hearings may precede drafting and introduction of a bill embodying committee decisions.

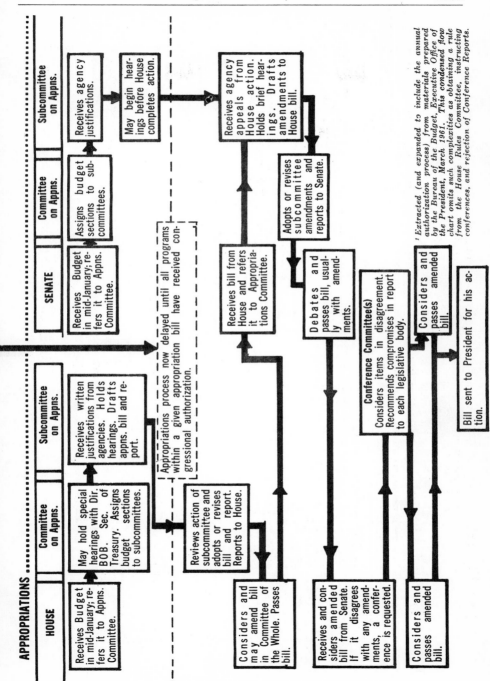

APPROPRIATIONS

Figure IV.   Staffs of the House and Senate Committees on Appropriations 1947-1963

	House Appropriations[2]					Senate Appropriations[3]				
		Regular Staff		Special Investigating Staff						
Year Months	Clerks	Clerk Steno. Others	Sub-total	gating Staff	Total	Clerks	Professional Staff	Clerical Assts.	Agents, Investigators	Total
1947 Mar	10	14	24	14	38	10	3	3		16
Jul-Dec	11	16	27	20	47	8	8	4		20
1948 Jan-Jun	13	20	33	47	80	12	8	5		25
Jul-Dec	15	15	30	12	42	6	8	5		19
1949 Jan-Jun	17	28	45	19	64	6	7	4		17
Jul-Dec	17	18	35	18	53	6	8	4		18
1950 Jan-Jun	17	16	33	40	73	6	6	5		17
Jul-Dec	18	17	35	31	66	5	6	4		15
1951 Jan-Jun	21	18	39	59	98	8	7	8	4	27
Jul-Dec	21	19	40	74	114	9	6	8	4	27
1952 Jan-Jun	22	23	45	87	132	6	9	10	3	28
Jul-Dec	20	16	36	68	104	9	9	11	5	34
1953 Jan-Jun	20	29	49	87	136	7	14	8	6	35
Jul-Dec	20	27	47	16	63	6	16	12	9	43
1954 Jan-Jun	21	29	50	34	84	8	17	12	7	44
Jul-Dec	20	31	51	21	72	6	16	12	7	41
1955 Jan-Jun	22	38	60	38	98	7	13	8	3	31
Jul-Dec	22	34	56	47	103	9	13	6		28
1956 Jan-Jun	22	36	58	49	107	8	13	6		27
Jul-Dec	21	35	56	34	90	11	13	6		30
1957 Jan-Jun	21	34	55	53	108	9	12	7		28
Jul-Dec	21	29	50	43	93	9	12	7		28
1958 Jan-Jun	23	34	57	45	102	8	13	7		28
Jul-Dec	21	30	51	33	84	8	14	7		29
1959 Jan-Jun	20	33	53	48	101	8	14	8		30
Jul-Dec	20	29	49	49	98					
1960 Jan-Jun	20	32	52	56	108					
Jul-Dec	20	35	55	42	97					
1961 Jan-Jun	19	41	60	47	107					
Jul-Dec	18	31	49	47	96					
1962 Jan-Jun	20	37	57	55	112					
Jul-Dec	20	31	51	53	104					
1963 Jan-Jun	19	31	50	64	114					

(Legislative Reference Service has not compiled statistics for Senate beyond 1959. See Footnote 1 below.)

[1] Extracted from Legislative Reference Service, Library of Congress, *Statistical Study on the Staffing of Committees of the House of Representatives* from January 1, 1947 through June 30, 1963, compiled by Margaret Fennel with the assistance of Susan S. Koppel and John S. Gosnell, November 1963; and, *Statistics on Senate Committee Staffs 1947-1959*, compiled by American Law Division, February 1963.

[2] Regular staff has been divided between a) Clerks and b) Clerk-Stenographers—Others. Between 1947-54 the following were assigned to these two categories: a) Clerks, Asst. Clerks, 2d Asst. Clerks, clerk to majority, clerk to minority, consultants: b) Clerk-Stenographers, Messenger File Clerk, Pages, Messengers, Jan-Messenger. Between 1955-1963: a) Clerk and Staff Dir., Asst. Clerk and Staff Director, Staff Assistants, Editor, Asst. Editor, Jr. Staff Assts. clerk to majority, clerk to minority, consultants: b) Clerk-Stenographers, Clerical Assistants, Messengers, Jan-Messengers.

[3] Regular staff is subdivided into four groupings. The following were assigned to these categories: a) Clerks: Chief Clerk, Asst. Chief Clerk, Asst. Clerks, Staff Member, Consultant, Counsel, Minority Counsel, Administrative Asst. Fiscal Officer, Staff, Staff Director, Asst. Staff Director, Research Asst. (i.e. all personnel and overhead other than, professional staff, agent-investigators and secretarial assistance); b) Professional Staff and Director (*only* those specifically designated "Professional" staff); c) Agents and Investigators (essentially the foreign aid investigating staff that was combined with the regular Appropriations staff from 1951—and which also is reflected in increases in a) and d) over the same period), and d) Clerical Assistants and Secretaries.

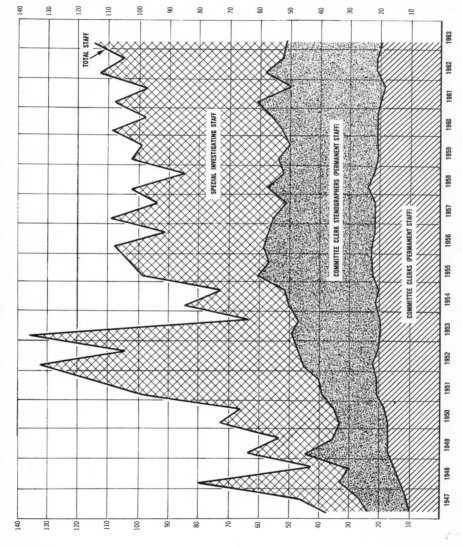

Staff of the House Committee on Appropriations (1947-63)

INDEX

Act of August 24, 1935, 51

Alaska, 13

American Bureaucracy, 176n

American Business and Publicity Policy, 176n

American Institute of Accountants, 153

American Political Parties: Their Natural History, 110n

American Political Science Association, 135n, 139n

American Political Science Review, 108n, 116n, 119n, 122n, 132n, 134n, 139n, 176n

American Presidency, The, 119n

Appropriations

  budgetary scorecard, 76-81

  Budget Information Service, 189, 190

  congressional budgetary process: availability of information, 189-192

  —congressional review, 41-52

  —criticisms, 129-141

  —forms of authorization and appropriation, 31-33

  —goals of, 176-179

  —historical development, 107-120, 122

  —points of control, 36-40

  —pressure groups, 5-23

  —procedures leading to congressional enactment of appropriation bills, 28-34, 120-127

  —reforms, 71-84, 143-174, 179-193

  congressional committee staffs, 151-160, 185, 188

  General Accounting Office: congressional utilization of, 144-151

  item veto, 31

  Joint Committee on the Budget: analysis of proposal to establish, 169, 174

  Joint Committee on Fiscal Policy: need for, 181-183

  legislative budget, 160-164

  omnibus appropriations bill, 164-169

Area Redevelopment Administration, 9

Arizona, 13, 86

Arms Control and Disarmament Agency, 55, 62

Atkins, Carter W., 169n

Atlanta, Georgia, 20-22, 86

Atomic Energy Commission, 48, 152, 173

Baker, John W., 123n, 167n, 182n

Banfield, Edward C., 134n

Bauer, Raymond A., 176n

Brinkley, Wilfred E., 109n, 110n

Bow Task Force, 139, 140, 188

Bridges, Styles, 162

Brownlow Commission, 119

Buchanan, James, 135n

Budget and Accounting Act of 1921, 72, 108, 114-117, 126, 144, 145n, 146, 151

Budgetary Process in the United States, The, 30n, 108n

Budget of the United States

  appropriations committees: staffs, 151-160, 185-188

  Atlanta, Georgia: federal expenditures in, 20-22, 86

  budgetary alternatives, 59-69, 88, 89

  budgetary scorecard, 76-81, 89

  budget concept: budget expenditures, cash payments to the public, and federal expenditures on income and product account, 81-84

  Budget Information Service, 189, 190

  budget message for fiscal 1964 (excerpt), 83

  congressional appropriations: apportionment of funds following enactment of, 34-36, 87

  —availability of information, 189-192

  —control of, 36-40, 86, 87

  —criticisms of budgetary process, 129-141

  —goals of budgetary process, 176-179

  —historical development of budget system, 107-120, 122

  —procedures leading to enactment of, 25-33, 36-40, 86, 87, 120-127

  —reforms, 71-84, 143-174, 179-193

  Congressional devices to control budget, 71-84

  congressional review, 41-52, 87-88

  cost information, 184

  Department of Health, Education, and Welfare: 1964 budget request, 42-45

  Department of the Interior: 1964 budget request, 45-47

  fixed-cost items: congressional and executive review, 49-52, 88

functional concentration of expenditures, 7-10
General Accounting Office: congressional utilization of, 144-151
industrial concentration of expenditures, 15-17
Joint Committee on the Budget: analysis of proposal to establish, 169-174
Joint Committee on Fiscal Policy: need for, 181-183
legislative budget, 160-164
national purposes upon which government programs are based, 60-66
1964 budget: detailed program composition, 95-100
—legislative proposals, 54-56
omnibus appropriations bill, 164-169
pressure groups, 5-23, 85, 86
regional concentration of expenditures, 10-15
trade-offs in expenditures, 61-69, 89
Bureau of the Budget, 28, 34, 35, 39, 86, 87, 109, 115, 116, 117n, 119, 124-126, 132, 137, 144, 148, 159, 170-172, 184n, 186, 189-192
Bureau of Labor Statistics, 20
Bureau of Public Roads, 27
Burke, Edmund, 176n
Burns, James MacGregor, 133n, 172n
Business Review, The, 26n
Byrd, Harry F., 118, 164

California, 13, 86
California Management Review, 68n
Campbell, Joseph, 114n, 145n, 146
Cannon, Clarence, 80, 81, 107, 127n, 137, 148, 149n, 152, 154n, 155, 156, 163-167
Carroll, Holbert N., 122n, 136n, 162n, 165n, 168n
Case, Francis, 163n
Chamber of Commerce of the United States, 79n
Charts
authorization—appropriations processes, 200, 201
budget process: components of, 198, 199
—major steps in, 196, 197
federal budget (1964): controllability of security—related and domestic—civilian programs, 50
House and Senate Appropriations Committees: staffing data, 202, 203
relation of authorizations to expenditures, 37

Civil Rights Commission, 56
Civil Service Commission, 152
Clapp, Charles L., 122n, 187n
Classification Act of 1949, 147
Clay, Henry, 113
Colm, Gerhard, 28
Colmer, William M., 154n, 155n
Commodity Credit Corporation, 32
Congress,
appropriations: availability of information, 189-192
—congressional goals, 176-179
—criticisms of budgetary process, 129-141
—historical development of budget system, 107-120, 122
—pressure groups, 5-23
—procedures, 29-34, 36, 39, 120-127
—reforms, 71-84, 143-174, 179-193
budget: congressional review, 41-52
—control devices, 71-84
—proposed congressional committees to control, 73, 74
—budgetary scoreboard, 76-81
Budget Information Service, 189, 190
committees on appropriations: staffs, 151-160, 185-188
General Accounting Office: utilization of, 144-151
Joint Committee on the Budget: analysis of proposal to establish, 169-174
Joint Committee on Fiscal Policy: need for, 181-183
legislative budget, 160-164
omnibus appropriations bill, 164-169
poll of members by Dartmouth Public Affairs Center, 150n, 164, 165
year-round sessions, 193
Congress and the Forces that Shape It: Legislative Politics U.S.A., 131n
Congressional Control of Administration, 131n
Congressional Control of Federal Spending, 30n
Congressional Quarterly, 139n
Congressional Quarterly Almanac, 140n
Congressional Reorganization: Problems and Prospects: Conference Working Papers, 150n
Congress: Its Contemporary Role, 151n
Connecticut, 13, 86
Control of Federal Government Expenditures: A Statement on National Policy, 181n

Council of Economic Advisers, 26
Curtis, Thomas B., 139n, 190n, 192n

Dartmouth Public Affairs Center, 150n, 164
Davidson, Roger H., 150n, 164n, 179n
Dawson, Raymond H., 122n, 141
Deadlock of Democracy: Four Party Politics in America, 133n
deCervantes, Miguel, 71
Democracy in the United States, 119n
Department of Agriculture, 7, 10, 21, 22, 31, 55, 56
Department of Commerce, 20, 22
Department of Defense, 7, 15, 21, 22, 48, 68
Department of Health, Education, and Welfare, 7, 20, 22, 41-46
    analysis of 1964 budget request, 42-45
Department of the Interior, 21, 45-47, 52, 82
    analysis of 1964 budget request, 45, 46
Department of Justice, 8, 67
Department of Labor, 47
Department of State, 8, 55
Dexter, Lewis A., 176n
District of Columbia, 13
Dworshak, Henry C., 157, 158

Eckstein, Otto, 65
Economic Analysis of the Budget, 72n
Education
    grants to A&M colleges, 31, 51
Employment Act of 1946, 118
Eulau, Heinz, 176n
Export-Import Bank, 55

Federal-Aid Highway Act, 27
Federal Aviation Agency, 20, 22
Federal Budget and the National Economy, The, 28n
Federal Bureau of Investigation, 20, 152, 153
Federal Power Commission, 152
Fellner, William, 108n
Fenno, Richard, 108n, 123, 126, 138n, 139n, 159n, 185n
Financial Management in the Federal Government, 145n, 147n, 163n, 169n, 184n, 192n
Fiscal and Debt Management Policies: A Series of Research Studies prepared for the Commission on Money and Credit, 108n
Ford, Gerald R., 139n
Frelinghuysen, Peter H. B., 139n
Frye, Alton, 122n, 141n, 184n

Gallatin, Albert, 109-111
Galloway, George 104, 109n, 112n, 124n, 154n, 161, 165
General Accounting Office, 109, 113, 116-119, 138n, 143-153, 155, 158, 170-172, 184, 186-188, 190
    congressional utilization, 144-151
General Services Administration, 31, 66
Good, James W., 115, 116, 117n
Government Corporation Control Act, 148n
Government of the Atom: The Integration of Powers, 139n
Grand Teton National Park, 52
Green, Harold P., 139n, 172n
Griffin, Robert P., 139n
Griffith, Ernest S., 151n
Gross, Bertram, 156n, 180n

Hamilton, Alexander, 109-111
Hammond, Paul Y., 108n
Harris, Joseph P., 18n, 28n, 59, 69, 131n
Harvard University, 131n
History of the House of Representatives, 109n
Holifield, Chet, 177n
Holman Rule, 114n
Hoover Commission, 119, 192n
House of Representatives and Foreign Affairs, The, 122n
House Rules Committee, The, 121n
Housing and Home Finance Agency, 20, 21, 22
Hugo, Victor, 1
Huitt, Ralph K., 108n, 135n, 156n, 176n
Huntington, S. H., 125n

Illinois, 15

Jacksonians, The, 112n
Jefferson, Thomas, 110-112
Jensen, Ben F., 174
Journal of Politics, 165n

Kansas, 13, 86
Kilpatrick, Carroll, 140n
Kirwan, Michael J., 133n
Klutz, Jerry, 140n
Kofmehl, Kenneth, 152n, 187n
Kovenock, David, 150n, 164n, 179n

Legislative Reorganization Act of 1946, 73, 104, 119, 144, 146, 148, 150n, 151, 152, 154, 156, 157, 160, 161, 168, 169, 181n
Library of Congress, 11, 12, 165n

Life Magazine, 132n
Lindblom, Charles, 135n
Lowi, Theodore, 131n, 132

Maass, Arthur, 132n
Macmahon, Arthur W., 120n, 126n,
    133n, 151, 155n, 156n, 157
Mahon, George H., 153n, 160n, 174
Maps
    Defense industries: percent of total
        manufacturing employment by
        state (1960), 14
Marx, Fritz Morstein, 116n
Mathews, Donald R., 123n
McCarl, J. Raymond, 146
McClellan, John L., 155, 168, 169, 173
McCormack, John W., 139n
McCormick, Medill, 117
McCracken, Paul, 76n
*Member of the House: Letters of a
    Congressman*, 123n
Miller, Clem, 123n, 167n, 182n
Monroney, A. S. Mike, 161, 162
Morgan Guaranty Survey, The, 165n
Mueller, Eva, 67n

National Aeronautics and Space Ad-
    ministration, 10, 48, 61, 184n, 193
National Association of State Cham-
    bers of Commerce, 153
National City Bank of New York, 153
Neilan, Edwin P., 132n
Nelson, Dalmas H., 165n
Neustadt, Richard E., 119n
New Mexico, 13, 86
New York, 15
Novick, David, 68n

O'Leary, Michael, 150n, 164n, 179n

Pennsylvania, 15
Pillion, John R., 139n, 140n
*Planning and Forecasting in the De-
    fense Industries*, 15n
Political Science Quarterly, 120n, 126n
*Politics of the Budgetary Process,
    The*, 108n, 124n, 135n
Pool, Ithiel de Sola, 176n
Post Office Department, 8, 21, 22, 31
President and Congress, 109n
Pressure groups,
    list of, 9, 10
Professional Staffs of Congress, 152n
*Public Administration and Policy De-
    velopment: A Case Book*, 132n
Public Administration Review, 18n,
    124n, 135n
Public Health Service, 43

Quarterly Journal of Economics, 67n

RAND Corporation Report, 254, 68n
Randolph, John, 112
Reorganization Act of 1939, 119
Review of Economics and Statistics,
    76n
Riker, William H., 119n
Robinson, James A., 121n
Rosenthal, Alan, 139n, 172n
Rossiter, Clinton, 119n
Rural Electrification Administration,
    10, 56

Saloma, John S., 73n, 122n, 141n, 184n
    article, *The Responsible Use of
        Power*, by, 103-203
Saltonstall, Leverett, 148
Schelling, Warner R., 108n
Schmidt, Emerson P., 72
Schlusinger, Gerald C., 146n
Schultze, Charles L., 189n
Schwengel, Fred, 139n
Small Business Administration, 9, 21,
    22
Smith, Howard, 184n
Smithies, Arthur, 30n, 41, 49n, 108n,
    113n, 120n, 122n, 131n, 133n, 135n,
    139n, 146n, 158n, 165, 181n, 188n
Snyder, Glenn H., 108n
Stein, Harold, 132n
Stockfish, J. A., 15n
*Strategy, Politics, and Defense Budg-
    ets*, 108n
Sugar Act, 31

Taber, John, 152, 153, 174
Tables
    budget (1964): detailed program
        composition, 95-100
    economic development programs, 64,
        65
    government operations, 66
    national security programs, 62
    program composition, 61
    public welfare programs, 64
    budgetary scorecard, 77
    Department of Health, Education,
        and Welfare: budget request
        (1964), 44
    Department of the Interior: budget
        request (1964), 47
    federal expenditures: by agency
        (1964), 7
        by state (1959-61), 10
    Federal Government payments to
        the public (1964), 8
    government agencies: budget re-
        quests (1964), 48

government contracts: national security and civilian (1962), 16

government spending: budget expenditures, cash payments, and expenditures on income and prodduct account (1962), 84

industries for which the Federal Government is an important customer, 17

new obligational authority (1964), 34

Taft Commission on Economy and Efficiency, 131n

Taylor, John, 113

Tennessee Valley Authority, 152

Texas, 13

The Common Defense: Strategic Programs in National Politics, 125n

The Congressman: His Work as He Sees It, 122n

The General Accounting Office: Two Glimpses, 146n

The Governmental Process: Political Interests and Public Opinion, 108n

The Legislative Struggle: A Study in Social Combat, 156n

The Spending Power: A History of the Efforts of Congress to Control Expenditures, 108n

Treasury Department, 7, 46, 115, 116, 145, 152, 153, 166

Truman, David B., 108n, 176n

U. S. Information Agency, 61, 62

U. S. Senators and Their World, 123n

U. S. Steel Corp., 153

Udall, Morris, 177n

Utah, 13, 86

Veterans Administration, 21, 22, 47

Virginia, 13

Wallace, Robert A., 30n, 137n, 138n, 144n, 148n, 149, 164, 166n, 167

Warren, Lindsay C., 146, 147n, 148n

Washington (state), 13, 86

Washington Post, 140n

Weaver, Robert C., 20n

Weidenbaum, Murray L., 15n, 26n, 133n, 137, 184n

article: *Federal Budgeting, The Choice of Government Programs*, by, 1-101

White, L. D., 112n

Wildavsky, Aaron, 108n, 124, 125n, 127, 130, 135n, 162n, 163, 179n

Wilmerding, Lucius, Jr., 108n, 110n, 114n, 131n, 145n, 188n

Woll, Peter, 176n

Yellowstone National Park, 52

Young, Marilyn, 28n